For Better

and

For Worst!

A Dramatic Testimony of a Couple Staying
Married Despite Having HIV/AIDS

Robert E. and Jerilyn L. Ward

ISBN 978-1-64492-336-8 (paperback)
ISBN 978-1-64492-337-5 (digital)

Christian Faith Publishing, Inc.
832 Park Avenue
Meadville, PA 16335
www.christianfaithpublishing.com

Printed in the United States of America

Words of Affirmation

This book contains a journey of a great man and woman of God. The acts and deeds are heroism (unconditional love). They gave their lives for the faith and consistently serving the Lord their God. Like all Christians heroes (displaying unconditional love), they have endured hardships and trials but demonstrated courage and faith when confronted with life. For Better or Worst is not always understood by the world, but it is never overlooked by God.

-Felisa L. Ward, Prophetess

In all things we are to give thanks unto our Lord and Savior Jesus Christ. One of the many things that my wife and I are thankful for is the incredible testimony of lives of Pastor & 1st Lady Robert and Jerilyn Ward! We met the Wards several years ago at a church service in Deerfield Beach Florida. Afterwards, during a difficult period of their lives we were blessed to be able to share into lives. It was during this time that the Wards shared their incredible testimony with us and our congregation at the Bread of Life Christian Center. What the Wards have endured in their marriage and family is an awesome display of faith, love, and strength in their God and each other. To see what God has brought them through is nothing short of miraculous! We are confident that their book will minister and bless all who read. We are truly thankful that the Father God brought the Wards into our lives for a time such as this! Be blessed all of you.

-Pastor George & Jestina Bowles,
Bread of Life Christian Center, Inc.

I have watched a love I have never known exude from my oldest sister. It is a love that we all can emulate. It is true, Agape love for her husband that has helped her to thrive and survive. It is the kind of love that God himself in the form of Jesus Christ His Son has tried to get the world to understand. To understand what is really meant by "The Love of God'" is truly liberating. Some people have never found this love, only the complete destruction that comes in the form of money, drugs, sex or music. When I learned my sister had been cursed with an incurable medical condition, my first instinct was to fall back on my earlier promises of "taking care of business" if she or my other sisters were ever hurt. But vengeance belongs only to The Lord, and any man exacting vengeance on his own terms will reap the rewards that follow. I love my sister with an all-encompassing love and it is that love that allows me to not interfere and to let her continue to do what she does.

-Little (Big) Brother Jerrard Mack

Dedicated To

To our wonderful children the Lord has seen fit to bless us with: Nicholas, Brea, and Jessica. We thank you for your love and support during all those very hard times. You have had moments when things got real tough there for a minute, but each one of you made the decision to love us as your father and mother anyway. You have seen and experienced things that most children your ages would not have been able to handle. Words could never express how your mother and I feel toward the three of you. And for that, we do honor you and we *love* you all very much.

Contents

Foreword

If you are going to read only two books this year, make sure one of them is *For Better and For Worst!*. *For Better and For Worst!* is the true story and living testimony of true love's strength to survive true disaster in any form, because of true sustaining faith in The True & Living God!

This couple, Robert & Jerilyn Ward are an example of *Living Faith*, and what it means to overcome adversity. They are parents and they are pastors, Creative and innovative. They have an amazing relationship with each other, and together have pursued an enviable intimacy with our Lord and King. Their indestructible commitment to God and to each other gave them access to "*be seated with Him in heavenly places…*" Little did they know the journey before them, pathways they and their family would face — catastrophes that can make or break you, challenges that could cause many whose faith is not so developed to give up, give in, walk away, or worse.

Without warning, Robert was diagnosed HIV Positive (Human Immunodeficiency Virus — yes, the virus that causes AIDS, Acquired Immunodeficiency Syndrome). READ THIS BOOK because their perspectives, thought processes, strategies, responses, nuances, determination, and faith in action will leave you momentarily speechless and permanently fortified that you, too, have been equipped to overcome! Our miracles may be many and varied, expressive, tangible or intangible, astounding recovery or quietly beautiful transition, but they are *MIRACLES* just the same. Embrace your miracles as you enjoy this growth tool!

Drs. Helena & Kennith Barrington
Metropolitan Cathedral of Truth
Havana, Florida 32333
850-539-1690

Acknowledgments

Jerilyn and I would like to take this time to first, *thank God* for His Grace and Mercy on our lives. If it were not for His continued blessings, guidance, love, and healing power on and in our lives, we would not be here today writing this book. For His Word and the prayers of the saints has more than kept us these seventeen years. We are alive today because of His promise to us as believers who accept Jesus Christ as our savior and the precious gift of the Holy Ghost. Without Jesus, we would not be here to pen one line in the pages of this book. We give him all the glory all the honor and all the praise. It has truly been "for better and for worst."

To all our family members at large: thanks to all of you. We thank you for your prayers and support given to us during those tough times. From the bottom of our hearts, *thank you*!

We can't forget to mention Dr. Mia Y. Merritt, author, publisher and book writer's consultant who sat down with us to embark on this incredible journey, July of 2011. You will forever have a place in our hearts because you helped us to get started. As well as a special thanks to Dr. Peggy Henderson Jones, an additional writing consultant and editor who unfortunately passed away suddenly in December of 2017.

And to *our friends* and *co-laborers* in Christ: wow! There are so many of you to *thank*. You know who you are and know what your contributions were to our life. We cannot give you the reward you deserve, but we can give you a few words of gratitude and God will bring the increase. THANK YOU, THANK YOU, THANK YOU! Your prayers have been answered: we are still here and we have answered the call. May God richly bless each of your lives.

Psalm 118:17: "I shall not die, but live, and declare the works of the LORD."

Introduction

Marriages today are failing throughout this country and in the world every single day; it's a sad state of affairs, no pun intended. But you know what makes it even worse? It has crept into the Body of Christ, the very place where the world looks for the standard of living.

What is it exactly that we are looking for when we say, "I do"? We make the decision to get married to the person we say we love and want to spend the rest of our lives with. Then stand in front of a group of witnesses to make a vow that this is the only person that I am committed to, and then change our minds later when the hard times come. Why then, do we make these sacred vows in the first place if we don't really mean them?

In today's times, it would seem that marriages are being used more and more as a test drive, without any true commitment to the one you made vows to. It's sort of like going to a car lot and test-driving a car. We take it out on the road for a spin, just to see how it feels, if fits us, or see how we look in it. We even drive it by our friends and family members to see what they think about it. "Should I keep it or take it back for another?" Or could it be that, for some of us, we already have it planned somewhere in the back of our minds that if this doesn't work out, there is always an escape hatch somewhere, an escape route, just in case. With the way the world is today, there is always another option. What is that old saying? "The grass is always greener on the other side." But I have a question; what would happen if we took better care of our own grass and leave other folks' yard alone? A little fertilizer here, trimming over there, and a little manicure every now and then. If we took the same amount of time and effort taking care of what we have as we do looking at what someone else has, we could live life a lot better. I really believe it's a feeling of inadequacy—what I have is not adequate enough for me, so I'll throw it all away and get something else.

For better and for worse, that's the vow, but it would seem, by the statistics of marriages today, that we really only want the better and not even consider or want to think about the worse; the richer, not he poorer; and in good health, not in sickness. If you haven't noticed yet, there is a play on words of *worse* and *worst* in the title of our book. I wonder, who sets the measuring stick or the bar for what is better or what is *worst*? What is the worst thing that can happen to make our marriages come to an end besides "'til death do us part"?

For some, the better is lots of money, material possessions, living in the best neighborhoods or house, sending our children to the best schools, having enough money to do whatever we want to do whenever we want to do it. But what is the worst that could happen for you to make the decision to leave or divorce your husband or wife: not lifting the toilet seat, squeezing the toothpaste in the middle of the tube, snoring, not enough money coming in, too much money coming in (temptation), in-laws, the death of a child, etc.? I guess that's why so many couples choose not to put that phrase into the marriage vows anymore. It just doesn't fit into the new way things are. It's the twenty-first century, right. We are expected to "evolve," and it's killing our marriages.

These days, we interpret love in a different way: "I love you if you love me," or "I love you if you're lovely," or "As long as you do what I want you to do," or "As long as you fit into my mold/box," or "I'll love you as long as you love me." But if the truth be told, we change, or do we? Could it be that the real us comes out as we get more comfortable and familiar with one another? Selah.

Growing Up

Growing up as a teenage boy in south Florida, I spent a lot of time daydreaming of what it would like when I got married when I grew up. What kind of husband would I be? My expectation was to become professional football player, because I played football throughout high school and was pretty good. I would buy my mom a new house and car and make sure she had the best doctors money could buy. I would find the love of my life, marry her, have kids, and live happily ever after. My wife and my children would love me deeply; they would not want for anything and would never have any of the tragic and disappointing experiences I had growing up.

I was born in Fort Lauderdale and partially raised in both Pompano Beach, Fort Lauderdale, and Plantation, Florida. My parents were Pastor Winton and Missionary Nancy Ward. I grew up with four other brothers. I am the middle son, the tallest. and the biggest of them all, which eventually proved to become a real problem to my dad as I got older. We moved around a lot growing up for whatever reason and still unsure way to this day. So, making close friendships was very difficult. Because in our early ages my dad was an evangelist, our time as children was spent in church, a lot. We sang in choirs from the time we could barely sing to young adulthood. I have no complaints about that whatsoever. We traveled to various churches for different events and meetings as being a part of the denominational church we grew up in. as I said before, we moved around a lot, but finally stayed in one place for me to spend my entire high school years at one school. That's where I was intro-duced to football.

By the time I was ending eighth grade, I was already six feet and 275 lbs., which was pretty big for a fourteen-year-old. My mom had signed my two younger brothers up for Little League football, but I could not play because I was too big, so I had to wait until I got to high school. I didn't play my freshmen year because my dad would not let me. He didn't want us playing football, but Mom was the one who got us in. Thanks, Mom!

Summer Harvest

I remember as a child, from the time I was around two years old until I was about eight years old, our family traveled every summer out of Florida. My dad and my uncle, his twin brother, were farm labor contractors. Meaning they were hired by farmers to help bring in the owner's crops. They would pick up hundreds of people from around Southern Florida, beginning late May and early June on buses headed for work. We're talking two hundred to five hundred people at a time. Their job was to oversee the workers on a daily basis as they brought in various vegetables and fruit. They were contracted each year to travel to a different state, whether it was Georgia, Virginia, New Jersey, etc., depending upon the demand or the assignment. It wasn't just black workers, but when you arrived, you would also find Hispanics and workers from other areas from around the eastern part of the country.

My brother's and I enjoyed the traveling, seeing different cities, people, and meeting new friends each summer. We considered it a big adventure for us and even going to summer school. While there, we lived on a multifamily community, which was set up with two rows of wooden houses that were up off the ground sitting on bricks. The roofs were tin, and when it rained, there was a rhythmic sound that, when heard, could soothe anyone's nerves. And you got the best sleep ever. None of the houses had inside bathrooms or showers, so when we, the children, took baths, Momma would boil water on the stove and pour it into a large tin washtub that sat in the middle of the small living room floor. Our house had only two rooms, one for our parents and the other for my three brothers and me. However, my oldest brother slept on the couch in the living room. There was a small living room/dining room combination, a kitchen with a small stove, and what we called back then an icebox, which was a box where we kept a big block of ice and an ice pick that Daddy would use to chip the ice to put in glasses for cold water. It was in lieu of what today's refrigerators are. The bathrooms or outhouses, as they were called back then, were located outside about fifty to seventy-five feet from the back of the living quarters. There were two outhouses, one for boys and one for girls. Both had a long bench that had six to eight individual holes cut into the top of them with lids. Farther back from there were the male and female showers, where the older teenagers and adults would go to bath. Every now and then, Daddy would allow our oldest brother, Jr., to take us back there to shower.

The camp seemed nestled in the middle of the woods, a cornfield, and other field where various kinds of vegetables were growing, waiting to be harvested. Acres and acres of green beans, onions, tomatoes, squash, bell peppers, butter beans, etc., that was just in New Jersey. There were Georgia peaches and pecans.

Stolen Innocence

I can vividly recall at the age of seven, being in the outhouse with one of my brothers. Our parents had often instructed us to always stay together. As brothers, we were never to leave one another behind; but on this particular day, after my brother was finished using the bathroom, he left me inside and walked out before I was finished. I was left there alone as one of the much older teenage boys of a family living in the camp entered the outhouse and locked the door behind him. He would come to the outhouse while we were in there and wait around until we were done.

The older teenager approached me and began to fondle me, putting his hand on my penis. He then took my hand and put it on his, holding it there without one word ever being spoken. I do not remember how long this lasted before someone knocked on the door. The older boy then stopped and walked out. I thank God that nothing more happened to me behind those walls that day than what did occur. As I reflect back, I realize that it was God's grace that had someone to knocked on the door before anything else occurred. I learned that the young man who had done this to me died of the AIDS virus sometime in the '80s. My father and mother have both gone on to be with the Lord, and neither of them ever knew that these things happened to me.

Little did I know how this experience would shape the rest of my life; a door had been opened. There is a spirit that is attached to this sexual act, and it looks for a way into the lives it comes in contact with. It's called perversion. Meaning, the process of improperly changing something that is good or the alteration of something from its original course, meaning, or state to a distortion or corruption of what was first intended. In my case, the spirit of perversion had been transferred to me in that bathroom that day, giving me a perverted way of looking at sex. I never told anyone what had happened to me, until years later.

But the story didn't end there. A few years after, my father and uncle stopped the summer contracting work, and they both became longshoremen in South Florida. We lived in a duplex, which my father owned, with both sides having two bedrooms and two bathrooms. He rented the other side out to various occupants. At the age of ten, I was introduced to pornography when I discovered my older brother's stash of magazines that he kept hidden underneath his mattress. I would go get the magazines and look through them every opportunity I had when my brother was not home. I mean, there it was, right there in front of my eyes—naked women. No clothes, in different positions, and even different nationalities. As I would look through the magazines, I would become aroused, things started moving around in my pants but I didn't know what to do with that feeling. Then I began to notice I started to become aroused even when I was not looking at the magazines. I started looking at girls differently. I would wonder if the girls I saw had the same things that the ladies in the magazines had;

my imagination went wild. As a young man, we are told that these types of feelings are natural. We were told that it was part of growing up, of becoming a man. The waking up every morning in a tent with my underwear stuck to my private area, a wet dream is what I learned they were later on. I had not been exposed to masturbation, so there was no release, yet. I was in middle school at the time, so that made it even worse because the school had a swimming pool and swimming lessons were part of the PE course. The guys had on our bathing suits, and so did the girls. Oh my God! Some of the girls wore one-piece and others two-piece bathing suits. Either way, me getting in and out of the pool without pointing was every difficult. My friends and I would take turns swimming underwater just to get a closer look before getting caught by either the girls or the PE coach. The spirit of perversion had begun to arise and crave satisfaction. My father never sat us down as his sons and talked to us about these types of things, so what we did learn came from the streets. I was never taught about the damage, both spiritually and psychologically, that sexual perversion could have on a person. It can become an all-consuming spirit that is never satisfied and permeates the very soul—the mind, the will and the emotions of the individual with whom it has attached itself to.

My mother was the instructor in our home growing up; she's the one who taught me about how a woman should be treated. She tried to teach me from both sides of the coin, the female point of view and the male point of view, which I know was difficult being on the opposite side of the coin. She would tell me that all women are not the same, and to not be so eager to give gifts while dating but to get to know the person themselves first, without all the benefits. Unlike today's philosophy, "I want to find a friend with benefits," you know, "What do I get out of the deal?"

Momma had to teach her four boys the best way she knew how because Daddy wasn't always around that much during those impressionable years. As a longshoreman, my father worked on the docks loading and unloading both cargo and cruise ships, so it took him away from the house working long hours; and sometimes we would not even see him for two, three, four days or more. Even when he went into ministry as an evangelist, it was the same thing.

What Momma couldn't teach us, we learned on our own, whether in school, from friends, and other outlets. I know that many of you can attest that learning off the street or from outside sources is not always the best way to learn life skills at a young age. But that's how it was and, sad to say, it is.

However, in all the dreams that I ever had as a boy and with Momma's teaching, I never saw or imagined myself cheating on my wife let alone contracting a deadly disease and transferring it to her. That was never a part of the dream. My God! I had become an adulterer. With everything that I saw in my household and contrary to everything that my mother taught me, the very things that I despised the most and held with such contempt in the life of the men I grew up around has come upon me.

Jerilyn: Growing up…well, let's talk about that. I was the eldest of five children, born to Willie Ruth Mack. I was born in Deland, Florida, at West Volusia Hospital. I believe my life started really simple. My earliest memories are of my mother always being there and taking care of everyone. When I had a nosebleed because the radiator heating system dried out my nose, my mother was there. When my brother pushed me off the stool he wanted and I got a big gash in my forehead, my mother was there. My mother was there for all these traumatic events in my life. But yet I still found it hard to communicate with her. Why are these the first thoughts I am writing about my growing up? Well, it is simple these are my first true thoughts. If we are all honest, the traumatic occurrences in our lives stay with us more than any other events. When we sit down and begin to think about our lives, the things that hurt us taught us, and therefore they are our first thoughts.

Communication for me as the eldest child was challenging. I was different from all my brothers and sisters and was frequently told that I was weird or strange. My mother groomed me to be a little parent in her absence. I was told that I was the oldest and so that meant my behavior had to be exemplary for the younger siblings. Talk about some pressure. So my growing up years were years of learning responsibility no matter how heavy the weight of it. My mother was rearing five children alone as my stepfather was in the armed forces and traveled extensively from assignment to assignment. We initially lived with my grandmother until my mother was able to get a "good job" in another city, then we moved. I don't know if my mother knew the pressure I felt; she had too much on her mind, mainly providing for us and making sure we were learning what we needed to learn.

I did not understand that all these things were shaping and molding me for my life. I cried a lot during these early years. Always yearning for a place to be alone and think. In a house with five children, there is no place to really be alone. So I escaped in books and listening to music. These times of escaping brought frustration to everyone in my house especially my mother. It brought frustration to everyone because they had to call my name so many times to get my attention. I also learned during these days that my life was not really mine but to be shared, even though I longed for time for just me. What really helped me was when I accepted Jesus as my savior when I turned thirteen years old. There was such a peace that washed over me when I sincerely prayed the prayer asking him to come into my life. I am thankful my mother took us to church. I now began to understand the struggles I had been having in my life, like the bad dreams and this yearning to know how we all got here, and what was the meaning and purpose for my life or just life, period. Many think that Jesus is for the weak. Well, they are wrong. You have to be strong to stand and believe in the Savior of the world while naysayers mock your faith. Once I accepted Jesus, a new journey began to take shape in my life, with new challenges and faith-building test.

The Marriage Vows

Dearly beloved, we are gathered together here today in the sight of God and this company, to join together this man and this woman in Holy matrimony. Marriage is an honorable estate, instituted by God, blessed by our Lord Jesus Christ, and declared by Saint Paul to be honorable among men. It is not, therefore, to be entered into without Holy counsel, or lightly, but reverently, soberly, advisedly, and in the fear of God.

"I, _____, take thee _____, to be my lawfully wedded wife, to have and to hold from this day forward, for better or for worse, for richer or for poorer, in sickness or in health, to love and cherish till death do us part, according to God's Holy ordinance, and thereto, I pledge thee my faith."

Robert: Now, I believe that God gave similar vows or commands to Adam and Eve in the very beginning of time as the first married couple to exist on earth. As the first set of man on the earth, Adam was given these instructions:

> And the LORD God said, It is not good that the man should be alone; I will make him an help meet for him. And out of the ground the LORD God formed every beast of the field and every fowl of the air; and brought them unto Adam to see what he would call them: and whatsoever Adam called every liv-

ing creature that was the name thereof. And Adam gave names to all cattle, and to the fowl of the air and to every beast of the field; but for Adam there was not found an help meet for him. And the LORD God caused a deep sleep to fall upon Adam, and he slept: and he took one of his ribs, and closed up the flesh instead thereof; And the rib, which the LORD God had taken from man, made he a woman, and brought her unto the man. And Adam said this is now bone of my bones, and flesh of my flesh: she shall be called Woman, because she was taken out of Man.

Therefore shall a man leave his father and his mother, and shall cleave unto his wife: and they shall be one flesh. (Gen 2:18–24, KJV)

Guys, could it be any clearer what our role is as husbands and our position beside our wives for the long haul? Adam and Eve both had their instructions to carry out that, if followed, would bring harmony to their relationship. Adam's job was to take care of the garden, name the animals, and stay in communication with God for instruction, but he needed help. Men, as much as we want to believe it, we need help. Adam had no one around who was like him or after his own kind. There was no one there for him to commune with physically. He could not produce by himself. God wanted there to be more of his kind (mankind), and they were to be fruitful and multiply and replenish the earth. That means when the population runs short, add to it, and you can't do that if the man and woman are not cooperating together.

Her position was to be, dare I say it, the homemaker who would take care of her husband first and the children. Now I know that this is not favorable statement these days, but think about it. That's the way it was not that long time ago, before the world changed.

And as for Eve, He said, *"Unto the woman he said, I will greatly multiply thy sorrow and thy conception; in sorrow thou shalt bring forth children; and thy desire shall be to thy husband, and he shall rule over thee"* (Gen 3:16).

Jerilyn: Now, ladies, let's be honest, after you read that scripture, you know something rose up inside of you. Like, "What! My desire shall be only to my husband? Wait a minute, what about my desires? Rule over me, what? Who? He will not have that much power in my life." Come on, let's be real here. When you read that scripture verse your flesh will cringe. God was not partial in his discipline. He gave Adam his marching orders, and this scripture defines what were Eve's orders because of her sin. None of us is exempt in this walk of being a Christlike example of Jesus and being His Bride.

Romans 8:28 says, *"And we know that all things work together for good to them that love God, to them who are the called according to his purpose."*

Well Adam and Eve were the firstborn, according to His purpose to create man. So God had to deal with their disobedience. So, ladies, no matter how much we hear about the women's liberation movement, etc., and whatever else that has been put out there, these are our marching orders: Gen 3:16: "Unto the woman he said, I will greatly multiply thy sorrow and thy conception; in sorrow thou shalt bring forth children; and thy desire *shall be* to thy husband, and he shall rule over them."

I have to admit, I didn't know my flesh had such a problem with this until I was married. When I was watching the married couples as a young woman, I wanted it so badly. I read the scripture in Genesis and thought, "Oh, I can do that Lord, I just want to be married," or the truth translation, "Oh Lord I just want me a man." Come on, let's be real—no matter how much we buck against scripture, it is showing us what our lives are and should be if we submit. Now in submitting, it will bring heaven on earth, but our minds get in the way; and the media images, which are contrary to God's word, have brainwashed us and have kept us from our piece of heaven.

Robert: I remember these words (the marriage vows) and I vowed to keep them. What happened to me? And how did I get to this place? I was asked to repeat these words to my wife-to-be, standing there in front of the man of God and before witnesses on that blessed day. I confessed with my own mouth that I understood the words that I was being asked to repeat and vowed to keep. What went wrong? How did I get so far off course?

Jerilyn was twenty-two years old, and I was twenty-seven years old. We were not that young getting married, so what is really going on? Again, how did I get so far off course?

Jerilyn: I don't know how my mind got to be so set that once you get married, that is it, but it was set. I stood in front of the pastor and repeated my vows, knees knocking and praying inwardly, "Lord please let this be the right man, *I do not* want to do this again." Robert looked so calm, and his eyes held such love. This was not the storybook wedding I had dreamed of, as we stole away or eloped to get married. My mother had not been very keen on the idea of Robert and I getting married, so that had put a strain on our seeing one another, so we decided to remove the strain. Thank God we were still getting married in a church; we had witnesses, a photographer, and our love for one another. Standing in front of the pastor that night I had no idea that this was my introduction to real life. You know what real life I am describing—the school of hard knocks. The type of knocks that take your breath away, cause you to cry all night, and make you want to scream while running to find a hiding place— those kinds of knocks.

The Beginning

It was around May of 1989, five months after the death of my mother (December 6, 1988), that I decided to move back to Daytona Beach. I was going back to the place where I found peace from all that haunted me, a place where I grew up. I decided once I left Fort Lauderdale that I would never come back; nothing else there mattered. The most important person in my life, my best friend, had left me and without anyone else to turn to. I packed up my mother's little red Hyundai that she had purchased months before her passing, which I took over the payments, and hit the road. I remember driving up I-95 with tears in my eyes, yelling at God and blaming him for taking her away from me, the only person on this earth that really understood me and who I was, and telling Him that I never wanted to hear from Him anymore. Furthermore, I didn't even want to be a Christian anymore. I know—crazy huh? It was a long hard ride, just trying my best to leave everything that was behind me in the past and setting my focus on a new life with new people.

I actually got saved in one of my dad's revivals when I was fifteen years old. I was the first of the children to become born again, even though we all grew up and participated in the church together. As I got older, I became hungrier for the word of God and wanted more than what I saw in church as a child. There had to be more to God and the Bible than Noah's ark, Moses and Pharaoh, Daniel in the lions' den, and the three Hebrew boys in the fiery furnace. I wanted more. So, after I got accepted to then Bethune Cookman

College, I hooked up with some of the guys in my dorm that were having a Wednesday night Bible study in the dorm study lounge. One night, September 16, 1981, I went in to see what they were discussing. I was hooked. They were talking about scriptures that I had never even heard of, and I understand what they were saying without all of the yelling and screaming. They actually taught from the word of God and made sure that you followed along with them. Afterward, the guy who was leading the study asked if there was anyone who wanted to give their life to the Lord. Before I knew it, my hand went up. I got myself ready to get on my knees and start calling Jesus, as this was the way they did it back home. But he asked the rest of the guys that was there to come around me then asked me to lift my hands and repeat after him. He led me into the sinners' prayer, and at that moment, there was such a peace that came over me. It felt like someone had poured cool water over me from the top of my head all the way down. For the first time in my life, I had peace. And that was the beginning of my walk with Jesus, the Lord of my life.

It was a tough time for me at first after returning to Daytona Beach. I started work at the Daytona Beach Marriott upon my return, as a transfer from the one in Boca Raton, and was able to start work right away. I lived with a couple friends of mine in their home, sleeping on the living room floor, for a few months until he helped me to find a place of my own. I worked in the mornings and had my nights off; that helped me to focus on other things other than my mother. Plus, I had lived in Daytona before, about two or three years prior, so it wasn't like I didn't know anyone. I just needed to reconnect with some of my old friends from college. There were some very good friends of mine, whom I had the privilege of being a groomsman at their wedding as well as attending the same college with that I hooked back up with and began to hang out when I could on occasion. They were both Christians, had two children, and going to church regularly, but I wasn't interested at that point.

The beachside apartment was pretty cool. It was more of an efficiency than anything else. It had one room with a bathroom, one queen-sized bed, and a closet for my clothes, which was positioned on the bottom floor of this old huge beach home with my own private entrance. I didn't have a kitchen or any appliances. All my food was kept in a large hard plastic ice cooler that sat on the floor at the foot of my bed; I bought it from one of the convenience stores down the street. That's how I kept my cold food cold (eggs, milk, cheese, sandwich meat, etc.). The unit also came with an AC unit that came out of the wall, which kept me cool in the summer, but I struggled for warmth in the winter. But it was mine! And that's how I lived for quite some time.

Everything was going so well for me as I became more settled in. Until one day while I was working, the sous chef came over to me and told me that I had a phone call, which we were not supposed to get while on the clock. So, I told him that I would make it fast. And as I answered it, the female's voice on the other in of the line sounded just like my mother's. She never said her name; she just started talking to me, asking me how I was doing and if everything was all right. I was too afraid to ask, "Momma, is that you?" So I just asked, "Who is this?" Then the she told me who she was. It was a dear college friend of mine that had heard of my move back to Daytona and was calling to check on me. It was all I could do to finish the conversation with her, standing there, leaning on the wall behind me. I ended the call by telling her that I would talk to her later because I wasn't supposed to take personal calls.

I got off the phone quickly and returned to work, barely able to get through my shift as I was shaking so much, trying to hold in my emotions. I called a friend and told her that I needed her to take a ride with me after I got off work; she agreed and asked me what was wrong. I told her that I would explain when I saw her. I drove to her house, picked her up, and drove to the nearest liquor store, bought a bottle of vodka and some cranberry juice. With tears in my eyes, I told her what had happened and that I needed something to help me to calm down and to take away the pain of the day. You know that never helps anybody but adds to the problem. She tried to talk me out of it by telling me that drinking wasn't the way to do that, but I wasn't hearing that and insisted. I asked if she would drop me off at home and take the car with her so that I would not try to drive it anywhere later on that night. She dropped me off and went home.

After she left, I went inside, closed the door behind me, sat on the side the bed, and poured me one cup of vodka and cranberry juice then drank it down. After that, I put the cranberry juice to the side and drank the vodka straight from the bottle. I don't remember much from that point. I woke up, to my knowledge, a day and a half later, half on the bed with the biggest headache I had ever had. I went to the bathroom, looked in the mirror, and there was a big gash in my head followed by a knot the size of a Ping-Pong ball. I took a much-needed shower, cleaned my bed, sat down, and called my job to make sure that I still had one, then looked up and told my mother that I would never do that again and have not in twenty-eight years.

With all of my heart, to this very day, I believe God spared my life. I gave the devil a wide-open door, the perfect opportunity to take me off this planet—but God.

Afterwards, I called my friend and asked her if she would pick me up and that I would drop her back off at her house. So while I was there, I told her and her husband that I was going over to my college buddy's house to talk with him so that I can get my life back right with God—because he knows where I've come from, where I've been, and where I'm supposed to be; he was that kind of a friend. And I'll never forget what she said to me when I told them that; she said, "I know what you need to do, just don't come back here trying to preach to us." Just like that. I smiled, gave them a big hug and left. I got to my destination, knocked on the door, and there he was, my friend Tony, standing there with this big smile on his face. I asked him if I could talk to him for a minute; he said, "Yeah, man, come on in." We sat down; he asked, "Do you want something to drink?" I told him no, that I was good. Then He asked, "What's up?" And I can't explain what happened, but it was like someone had opened up a floodgate, and I just started telling him everything that had happened to me while I was gone all this time from Daytona, how things transpired with the passing of my mother, and what I had told God on my drive back here. But all he did was sit there, with this big grin on his face, not saying a word until I was done. Then after he made sure that I was finished, he said, "Let's pray," and he did. He prayed the simplest pray I'd ever heard and then asked me if I was ready to give my life back to the Lord. I told him yes, and he led me in the sinners' prayer, and I felt the Lord fill me with the Holy Ghost again. It was a new beginning.

We stayed in contact with each other after that. That's when he and his wife invited me to come to the church they had been attending and were working as part of the ministry team. I told them that I would if I could get a day off when they had their midweek service. Now, it was a while after that before I got the opportunity to keep my word, but I did visit with them quite a bit in the meantime, reestablishing our relationship and even babysitting for them if they wanted to go out on a date for themselves. The kids and I got along very well; they were the most interesting children that I had ever seen, on the good side.

One night, somewhere around the beginning of 1990, after getting settled back into the groove of things, I finally got a day off and decided to go to one of their church's Wednesday night services. I thought that I would surprise them by just dropping in on them. As I walked up to the church facility and rounded the corner, I could see the area where they had the children's ministry. Through the window, I could see their kids inside a class with all the other children and a young girl leading them in singing and taking care of them while the adults were in their own church service in the other part of the building. I visited the church several times after that, and I would get there the same time they did, so I could walk the two kids back to the children's ministry. The same young girl would always be there to greet them as they came in. She was so full of energy, and the children seemed to like her just as much as she liked them. I finally got up the nerve to ask them who this young girl was and how old she was, I figured she was at least seventeen or eighteen years old, maybe less. He told me that her name was Jerilyn, she was twenty, and that she and her entire family attended the same church. Well, I said to myself, "I'm twenty-five, man, that is too young for me. I need someone a lot older than that," and that was it. I did not mention her or say anything else from that point on. My mother would watch me all the time, especially when I got older. She would say to me, "Robert, you're different from your brothers. You like things that regular black people don't like, and it separates you from the crowd. Don't be ashamed because you like opera or ballet and all those types of things. That's what makes you, you. I wouldn't be surprised if you ended up marrying an older woman or someone white." Growing up, I did know of anybody my age or color that was interested in the things that I like, or maybe I was too shamefaced to ask.

Jerilyn: I have always been a highly energetic person and working in a children's church was right up my alley. The children's church pastors needed help, so I volunteered. I was working one night, and in walked this tall muscular young man holding the hands of the Children's Pastors' children who were around three and four years old. My mind wrestled with the thought. He must be kind and gentle; otherwise, these two kids would have not been walking with him. I wondered who he was but never asked because the Children's Pastors seemed to have complete confidence in him. I didn't see him for a while after that, so who he was remained a mystery.

Robert: I'm taking this time to tell you a little bit about the beginning of our relationship so that you can see that things don't always start how you think they would. We are the ones that take life and one another for granted and then wonder what happened and how things got the way they did. There are distractions that will come in everyone's life, but you have to recognize them as such and find some kind of way to get yourself back on track.

I met up with Jerilyn again around the fall of 1990. I was twenty-six, and she was twenty-one at the time, at the Bible study that a mutual friend of ours started in the living room of his and his wife's apartment; she came one night to visit along with her mother and the rest of her brothers, sisters, as well as her aunt and cousins. All one big happy family is what they appeared to be. I worked the sound board, helped set up chairs, and whatever was needed for my friend to get this ministry off the ground.

Jerilyn: The mystery has been solved. This gentleman is a man of God. Lord, could this be the one? My heart skipped a beat this particular night at Bible study. I had been watching Robert and thinking what a strong humble man to serve this couple as he does. He washed dishes, clothes and babysits their children. Where do you find a man like that? Lord, is he the one? I sat with him this particular night and began to share some intimate details about my family, and His reaction to the information surprised me and brought me peace. He did not flinch or shy away from what I shared.

Robert: We began to become close friends, as we hung out together and spent time talking with each other. Then it happened. One night, Jerilyn came over to talk to the pastor alone. I was there because at that time, I had no place to live, and they put me up until I found my own place. Okay, back to the story. After their meeting, Jerilyn needed a ride home, as the buses didn't run after 7:00 p.m., and she had no other way home. I was the only one available at that moment with a car, so I drove her home. On the way, I began to ask her about herself. This was something new to me, but I went for it. She began to share things with me that I did not know any young lady would be that comfortable telling someone they just met. I sat there listening attentively to everything that she had to say, wondering why she was telling me all this stuff. She didn't know me like that, but it was okay—that's all I can say: "It was okay."

I pulled up into the driveway of her mom's house. She said that it was nice talking to me and thanked me for the ride, then she got out and walked to her front door. I believe it was her mother that opened the door and let her in. I said good night and backed out of the driveway and said to myself, out loud, "Lord, I'm going to marry her, huh?" Just like that, I asked God a question; and just like that, he answered.

That was September of 1990.

Jerilyn: I got out of the car that night fairly shaking. When my mother opened the door, I rushed in the house, greeted her, and went straight to my room. Sat on the side of my bed and began questioning God again. "Lord, I don't want to do anything outside of your will. I've wanted to be married so bad, is this just me? UGH!" Come on now my heart is racing and my mind—needless to say, I did not sleep much this night. When awakened the next morning, I went on the hunt looking for a list that I had written of what type of man of God I desired to be married to. I had attended a conference, and they had a singles' meeting. And in that meeting, they encouraged the singles to write a list. They also encouraged each single to be mindful of asking for what they wanted and not being prepared to compliment the weakness of their desired spouse with strengths that we must develop in Jesus.

I found the list and again the shaking began in my body. Robert matched the list, except for two items. My mind began to race with half prayers and half questions: God could this be after all this time of waiting? Is Robert my husband? I had not felt this way about any man. I had had my crushes and puppy love, but Robert created a longing in my soul that made me a little dizzy. Just the sound of his voice after the realization that this could be it, the one I have been waiting for, caused my knees to buckle. Such moments are sweet trauma to the soul—aww, love…it buds and sweeps you off your feet.

I had never felt like this before, where within me a calm assurance began to grow that yes, this was to be my husband. To be sure, I took three days to fast and deny my flesh by seeking God's will and direction. Still, the answer came back a resounding yes. Now this was just me and God having this conversation. Then I told my family, and it seemed that no one else was hearing God. My mother was not keen on the idea at all. She and I had had occasions where we did not see eye to eye, but this time seemed to bring such trauma to my soul and my world. You can understand why; everyone wants their family to be excited when they find their mate, correct. This was not to be my path to marriage. From that point on, our atmosphere at home, for me, was tense. I began to just go to work, come home, do my chores, and spend time in my room reading, listening to music, or sleep. When it was time to go to church, I would wait outside for Robert or the pastors to pick me up to avoid any confrontations with my mother. Robert and I begin to spend a lot of time together, mostly running church errands and riding and talking,

talking, talking. We begin to make plans for our life and discuss what we were looking for in marriage. Now, in all of this, my flaws were yet to show. Several flaws in my character and personality brought reality down on us before even getting married. Being raised/reared in a single-parent household and being the oldest made me a very forward young woman who was not used to following male authority in any shape but a pastor who was only seen at church during services. The first challenge was my thinking that Robert was taking too long to tell my mother we were getting married. I pushed him to set a time and come and tell her of his proposal to marry me. He did, and the night we were sitting there, Robert was taking his time to explain his heart to my mother, who from my view really didn't care. It was so kind, all the details he was sharing about how he felt about me. But the entire time, I was sitting there like, "Hurry up and tell her." Well, that rumbling got to be too much in the pit of my stomach, and I interrupted and said, "Mother, Robert and I are getting married." She was, as I already knew, not happy or in agreement with this at all. Little did I know this was going to be a painful memory for my future husband. Now on to the next incident revealing more of the character flaw. Robert and I planned our engagement dinner, and we were on our way to the dinner when I had an emotional breakdown. This breakdown was because I did not have an engagement ring to show the people we had invited to the dinner, and I was feeling embarrassed like this would subtract from our engagement dinner. I kept asking him if we should cancel and go home until we had a ring. I did not know again how much pain I was causing my future husband. So much pain until he had to reveal to me that he had the ring with him. This revelation spoiled the surprise he was planning, which was to present the ring to me at the engagement dinner with all those who were in full support of our marriage. These types of interactions would not have occurred, I believe strongly, if there would have been a father/male authority in our house on a daily basis. With male authority in a house, day-to-day interactions with a man would have been displayed in front of me as a daughter, and learning the ways of a wife would have been displayed, but that was not the case for me.

So here I am, this young woman, married and struggling in her marriage. Now we are adding children to our lives. Nicholas was our firstborn, then Brea, and finally Jessica. They were all born back-to-back, three years in a row. Nicholas was born in February of 1993. I was twenty-four years old, and Robert was twenty-nine. Then Brea was born in January of 1994, and Jessica was born in January 1995. All three of the children were born healthy—what a blessing straight from heaven. The children brought joy with each birth, and I was thankful for such wonderful distractions from the painful challenges we were having in our marriage. It is true; we must admit that is what happens in some marriages: the children become a distraction, and they are the glue that holds us together in many cases. Wives, we really do this much more than husbands do. We get busy nurturing the children and focusing on taking care of them, and we begin to thrive in this area, and we have some renewed joy in the marriage. I did not think I would be happy to have children after being the oldest of five. I had said out of my mouth many times, I have already been a parent all my life, I don't know if I want to have children. But in those famous words of Shakespeare, "Oh thou dost protest too much." I wanted children of my own so that I could raise/rear them differently from the way I was brought up—you know, with two parents in the home, two cars, a house, a good job and a dog. Oh, what a pleasant dream. But the reality is, marriage is hard work. As we are progressing in our marriage, things are staying broken and not getting fixed. We go day by day with this routine of life and not really talking about the underlying issues we each are having. You know how we are as humans do; we find a place inside of ourselves and say, "This is okay, how I am living. It will get better soon." The life of denial, or simply lying to ourselves, because we are holding on to the dream or the fantasy, to be more accurate. Women, we carry things; and that goes for everything—children, disappointments, hurt, pain, incidents and snapshots of every traumatic event in our lives. So here we are, married, and the womb of my life is getting filled up. The children are growing up; we are still living out life day by day, paying bills, trying to find better jobs, going to church, working in the ministry—*ugh*! It was all so mundane but comfortable.

ROBERT E. AND JERILYN L. WARD

That sounds crazy, right? But how many of us do this, hoping our lives will change? For me, I wasn't just hoping but praying desperate prayers almost every moment. Cries of "Why me? Help! Lord, when is this going to get better? Who can I talk to about all this? Lord, do you hear me? This is not how my life was supposed to be. Lord, I am Christian, my life should be better than this. Is this it, Lord?" We have been married over nine years now, is it about to get better?

Bacterial Meningitis

The Beginning of the Worst

Waking up early that Sunday morning with a pounding headache, so much pain from an inner ear infection, I got dressed for church with the rest of my family so that we would not be late. The pain was so excruciating that I could not think, I thought that I would literally pass out. With bloodshot eyes and full of tears, we made it to church and walked in, with Jerilyn walking beside me every step of the way so that I would not fall. We sent the kids to their spot with the youth, and we took our regular place in the main sanctuary, fourth row from the front, where there were fewer distractions. As the service began with the praise and worship team, the music seemed louder than ever before, and it seemed to pierce to the very core of the nerve center of my brain. I thought that I would lose my mind. I thought that if I would just focus on praising and worshipping God and sing loud enough that I would forget about the pain that I was feeling; it didn't happen. Then to make matters worse, because there were empty seats on the front row, we were ushered up front to fill in, and all I could think of was, "Lord, please help me get through this." With tears running down my face, pain shooting through my ear and head, I lifted my hands and sang as if nothing was wrong; only Jerilyn knew what was going on with me. By the time we got home, I was in so much pain, grabbing my head, tears streaming down my face. I ran to the door and into my room. The only thing that I remember after that is stripping out of my clothes and getting into bed.

Jerilyn: Robert was in pain the entire service. It was very hard to enter into the service knowing that he was in this kind of pain. He had always given that "Oh, I am a man I can handle this" to everything, "I'll be all right, let's just go to church." So between praying in the spirit and numerous side glances, for my natural peace of mind, I sat through church. After church, Robert was in such excruciating pain that he became very irritable with the whole family. I left his side to pick up the children from children's church as quickly as I could, which was a job because I had to leave him in order to do that. In the past, when he had had ear infections, he would become off balance and was prone to falling, so of course, my anxiety level was high. We got in the car, and the children were excited, and they were talking loud, and Robert yelled at an unusually loud tone of voice for them to be quiet. And immediately after he yelled at them, he yelled from the pain in his ear. I whispered to the children that it was okay and to sit back and be quiet until we got home. We got home. I fixed dinner, got everyone fed, and then went to the store to get Robert some pain medication. He had been using Aleve and, in a moment of coherency, asked me for some pain medication. When I got back, I gave Robert the medication and then began the long night of Robert being off and on in the bathroom, screams from excruciating pain, and sickness that was seemingly never ending. Needless to say, I did not sleep this night.

Robert: I remember later that night, going in and out of the bathroom with diarrhea and vomiting on the hour every hour and the last time was around two o'clock Monday morning, sitting there saying to myself, "I got nothing left, I got nothing left" over and over again. The next thing I remember was waking up in the hospital Wednesday morning.

Jerilyn: Robert went into the bathroom this last time, and the pit of my stomach was tied in knots by this point, wondering what was wrong with him. I acted like I was asleep so that he wouldn't think he was keeping me up. It was now 4:00 a.m., and I had been lying there, talking to the Lord and praying for direction the whole night. Then it happened. I had just dozed off into a light sleepy haze when I heard what I thought was Robert choking. I was yelling his name, "Robert, are you all right?" But he did not respond, so I pushed him out of the bed onto the floor, onto his stomach, because I thought he was choking. (There was definitely an adrenaline rush because Robert weighed 335 lbs. and I weighed 125 wet.). He hit the floor and was wedged between the bed and the nightstand where he lay thrashing violently. I did not know what to do.

I got on the phone and called 911. I gave them the directions to the house in such a calm voice it frightened me. Thank God for his Holy Spirit. The paramedics arrived and took over, but they did so with a fight from Robert. So I had to get on the bed and literally sit on top of him and hold his arms so that he would not fight them as they ran the necessary tests to see what was wrong with him. Robert was looking wide-eyed and incoherent. The paramedics kept calling his name to get him to respond to his name. His responses were very lethargic and not enough for their comfort. The entire time this was going on, our children were sleeping; they did not wake up until the paramedics were ready to take Robert to the hospital. I brought them out to see their dad off to the hospital; by this time, our neighbors were slowly coming into the door to see if we were okay. They promised to pray for us; this brought tears to my eyes briefly. After the entire process of working on him, these were my first tears.

After the paramedics drove off, one of our neighbors asked if he could pray for us. I said yes; we all joined hands, and he prayed for Robert then us as a family. I quickly got the children dressed and went to the hospital. The children were still sleepy, so they began to lie on the chairs in the hospital with their eyes full of questions. I had managed to grab some grapes out of the refrigerator for them to eat, so I quickly gave them some as we waited. I checked several times for information on Robert's condition and asking the nurses to look after my children. I asked that they let me know something because

I had to take them home to get dressed for school. Even during this time, my mind was racing to keep order in our lives.

It was now 6:00 a.m., and time seemed to be moving ever so slowly. They didn't have Robert stable, yet so I took the children home and got them dressed and took them to school. I assured them that everything was going to be okay and that I would be there to pick them up when school was out. In the process of driving them to school, I called my job and let them know that I would not be there, that my husband was in the hospital and I would call them later with his status. I also called one of the assistant pastors from the church that we were attending, and he immediately prayed with me and let me know he would be by to check on us.

When I got back to the hospital, I immediately went in to see Robert and get the status of his condition. He was strapped to a bed, and there was no one with him. This momentarily disturbed me, but before I could say anything, the nurse appeared. She began to tell me what Robert's condition was, to the best of her knowledge until the test results came in. She then began to tell me that they would need to do a spinal tap as they wanted to thoroughly search for the cause of Robert's condition. She explained to me that he had had a seizure due to the result of him having a body temperature of 104.6 degrees. She finally explained that Robert was strapped down so that he wouldn't injure himself and others. The nurse then began to usher me out of the room because they needed to do a spinal tap to draw fluid from his spine to be tested, I told her no, that I would stay. Within me, I could hear a recent conversation that my sister and I had had about making sure you stay with your loved ones while they are in the hospital; otherwise, they could get treated badly. She had also told me that they tell you to change your visiting times frequently, especially if they have an extended stay. So I helped them keep Robert calm and talked to him so he kept his focus on me until the procedure was done. They continually tried to roll Robert over into position in order to do the spinal tap, but to no avail. Robert was going to lie where he wanted to lie. The position he ended up in was on his left side with his right arm hanging over the railing of the bed. The doctor said, "Let's just let him stay there, we can do it from here."

Shortly after the procedure Pastor Doug walked in the room. He spoke to me in soothing tones and assured me that everything would be all right. He prayed over Robert and with such a petition that I felt like angels were in the room with us. THANK YOU, Jesus! God always knows who to send and when to assist us in the times of our *greatest* Need. He left shortly after the prayer but assured me that if I needed anything to let him know.

The hospital staff then came back to move Robert to a different trauma room and to give me the results of his initial tests. Once Robert was settled in his room, the doctor let me know that Robert had bacterial meningitis. He said we should be thankful as the viral version of meningitis would have meant that we would have had to contact everyone that attended church with us on Sunday morning, which would have been close to four thousand people, to let them all know that they had been exposed to the virus.

After the doctor finished, I called my job and then began to call family members: Robert's dad, his brothers, my mother, my sisters and brothers. It seemed liked time was standing still while my mind was rocking and reeling. Robert flowed in and out of consciousness as we waited for a room; he had been admitted to the hospital.

He would ask me the same questions over and over again. "Why am I here?" "What's going on?" "How did I get here?" He would try to get out of the bed to go home, and I would have to coax him to lie down, sometimes with physical force. So much compassion welled up in my heart for him as he was in excruciating pain and not able to get any coherent thoughts together. As a wife, you go into the nurturing mode so there I was straightening the bed, putting ChapStick on his lips because they would get so dry, and checking with the nurses to see when the room would be ready and praying under my breath, asking for God for his help. Robert would wake up and ask me for something to eat and some water, but he couldn't have anything until they were able to get him stable again. He kept asking until I gave him a small sip of water.

We finally got a room, so I gathered what belongings Robert had and followed the nurse to the room. Robert's room was in the intensive care unit as he was still in danger because his fever was still high and spiking off and on. Once he was settled and sleeping, I went and picked up the kids from school. As I left the hospital, I started getting phone calls from family members asking about Robert's condition. I sat in the parent pickup line and let each one know his condition while I waited for the kids to come outside. In between calls, I would shake my head to stave off the feeling of numbness that was trying to overtake me. I felt like if I shook my head in the natural, it would help me stay clear for what I needed to do next. For someone who had learned to be real organized, this was chaos, and I had no control over it and could not organize anything but myself. Not a good feeling.

The children came outside, full of questions regarding their dad's condition—was he home, were they going to see him…? I answered those I could without upsetting them, and the rest I let just run on by for later. I took them home got them a snack and started on their homework. During this time, my brother-in-law called me back to ask how he and my youngest sister could help. He offered to come get the kids for the night so that I could stay at the hospital with Robert. I said okay and then went to get one night's worth of clothing packed for the kids. I was grateful for the help but at the same time feeling overwhelmed with this new chore to do. After my brother-in-law got the kids and assured me they would be fine and that He would bring them back tomorrow, I got a shower and got dressed finally and went back to the hospital. I just walked around his room, prayed out loud, and read the Bible out loud. I read scriptures about healing, but mostly I read scriptures that had encouraged us both in the past that had nothing to do with healing (Isaiah chapter 62:5, Psalm 107:20, Isaiah chapter 53). The numbness was really starting to close in on me. I could not fight it; there was nothing physical for me to do, and it overtook me. "God, what is going on?" was the cry in my mind and heart. The ICU nurse assigned to Robert's room was a little perturbed with me because I wouldn't wear a mask to enter his room. I told her what was the sense in that when we had been sleeping together every night for weeks; whatever I was going to get, I already had it at this point. I stayed as long as they let me, then I went home to do what could not be called sleep at all.

My first waking thought, "Lord what do I do now? Whatever this is, it's going to be for a minute, Robert is not even conscious, yet. Now his family is on their way, what do I tell them? We don't even know each other very well." So many thoughts raced through my mind. I got up, got dressed to go to work, then called to let them know I was coming; they firmly told me not to come in and to take care of my husband and children.

Why do we do this kind of craziness as humans? We worry about things that we should not even be concerned with. Here I was, worried about losing my job, and my husband was severely ill. The numbness/shock had really taken over. I went on to the hospital; same scenario as the day before—sat in his room, paced, prayed, and read the word out loud. People that knew him began to visit. My brother-in-law called and he was on his way with the children, so I went home to try to rest while I waited. Robert's brother called; they were on their way from Georgia, and he said Robert's dad was coming to. "Lord, please give me strength. How can I do this without my husband?"

Robert: As I woke up, looking around the room to see where I was, I felt around the bed, touched the cold railings, the gown I had on, and the lights that were shining from the x-ray panel on the wall—I needed to go to the bathroom real bad. Still out of it, I tried to go right there, but nothing was coming out; there was something blocking the flow, so I reached down to find out what was going on, and I began to pull and then yank the obstruction. By that time, I heard a voice yelling to me firmly, "Mr. Ward! Mr. Ward! No, No, don't do that!" There stood this lady in white, grabbing my hands and telling me that I had a catheter in and I could not remove it. She began to ask me if I knew where I was and how I got there. I answered her no on both questions and told her that I needed to use the bathroom. She told me that I could not get up yet, but she would remove the catheter and give me a urinal to use from the bed.

After I had gotten done, I was lying there on my right side with my hand hanging over the bed rail, looking at the bright x-ray light on the wall, when I heard a voice that was so loud I thought that there was someone in the room with me. Now, I must say this, I am not the type of person to go around saying I heard the voice of God or God told me this or that because I've seen the bad side of that and the damage it caused from those who used it as a way of drawing people to them. But I heard this: "This sickness is not unto death." Just like that; no more, no less. By that time, Jerilyn had come into the room and was asking me how I was feeling. I asked her what happened and why was I in here.

Jerilyn: Robert woke up full of questions and surprised that two days had already passed and he had no remembrance of either of them. All the while I was wondering how to feel, what to say. Here I was, my husband had been incoherent for two days, I had been entertaining his father, brother, and brother's family who I don't know very well; and my kids spent one night in Daytona with my sister and brother-in-law; and my son was acting up because his father is not around. What a whirlwind in a few days.

So I calmly answered his questions. I explained to him that he had bacterial meningitis and that he had a seizure. I told him how the doctor said if he hadn't had the seizure, we wouldn't have known that he was so severely ill as he was and he could have died within the next twelve (12) hours or so. This was really sobering information for the both of us. I also told him that when I got home earlier that day, and I realized I had not purchased Aleve for his pain but Advil. I told him that I believed that saved his life as Advil helps to bring fevers down. That in itself was a miracle. I let him know that his dad and brother were there and had already been to see him, but didn't stay long. He wanted to know why are they were there, was he dying or something? I said, "No, no, they are just here to see about you." He said he vaguely remembered his dad standing over him with his brother and sister-in-law, and he was praying. Robert said he began to think, "Am I dead or am I dying?" His responses were puzzling to me, as this was his family and they were here to see about him. I asked him if he was ready to see the kids as they were in the lobby. I brought them in to see their dad—no face mask. They stood back for a few minutes; they were not certain if they could get close to him or not. Robert assured them that he was okay and asked them to behave themselves and not to give me a hard time. Robert's energy began to leave him, and he motioned for me to let them go back to the waiting room.

By this time, I was exhausted, my emotions were spent, and I wanted all this to just be over. Robert's brother (Cleveland) his wife (Lisa), me, and the children all went back to our apartment so we could all eat. Lisa, Cleveland's wife, was concerned about me and she asked me what they could do to help me. I told her I really didn't know, but thanked them for coming down to see Robert.

Robert: I spent over two weeks in the hospital being poked and prodded, having temperature spikes as my body would shake uncontrollably because of the fevers and having to be cooled down with bags of ice all over my body to keep my temperature down, it was crazy. The doctor had ordered an ear specialist to come in to check my hearing, because the meningitis affects other parts of your body and could cause some memory loss also. The young lady came in to do the procedure. After she was done, she informed me that there was damage to my inner ears and that it was progressing and that I would experience hearing loss, and after a few years, I would be deaf. I did not react to her statement, and she was surprised; then she asked me if I was a Christian, I told her yes, and she proceeded to tell me that she was on the prayer team of one of the larger churches in the area, and that she would put my name on their prayer list, and they would keep me in pray for healing. Then she left, just like that. God knows, I said to myself and my wife later on that God had sent me an angel to comfort me.

The temperature spikes continued to happen right up until the last day that I was to be discharged. The doctors could not figure out what was causing the temperature spikes, so they ordered one more blood test. He asked my permission to do an HIV test so that they could rule out all other options. I told him yes; I wasn't worried about that that was the least of my worries, so I thought. They took the blood and released me to go home, and the doctor said that they would see me in a week for the test results.

Coming Home

W hen we got home, Robert walked in slowly and sat down. He had not been home for sixteen days, and everything seemed a little strange to him. The kids were standing back, waiting to see if and when it was okay to talk to him. I was thankful to not have to go back to the hospital again and that the whole family was now back in one place. This had been the longest two weeks of my life. Robert had trouble adjusting. He looked at himself in the mirror and began to break down. I called Pastor Doug again, and he talked with Robert and prayed with him.

We are all surrounded by people who can help us if we allow them to. We have to know that when we serve God, he looks after us completely. I thank God for an associate pastor who was willing to step in and help us in our time of need. I was spent in my energy at this point and so glad that he was available and willing to help.

Robert: Going into the hospital, my weight was 335 lbs.; when I left, it was 250 lbs. This may not mean much to anyone else but for me, this was a significant loss of weight. I haven't been 250lbs since I was 15 year's old being 6 feet tall. By the time I was a senior in high school, I was 6 foot 3 inches tall and weighed 340lbs. For me, I was Anorexic. I was very weak, my clothes were hanging off of me, my face was sunken in, and when I looked in the mirror, I began to weep bitterly and told Jerilyn, "That's not me, that's not me." To me, I looked like a dead man. I could barely stand on my own without shaking. I was a mess. Jerilyn got in contact with Pastor Doug, and he talked to me and prayed for me until I had calmed down and was able to talk back to him. I told him that I had looked at myself in the mirror and was overwhelmed by what I saw. I didn't know the man in the mirror. But as we talked, he was able to share with me what I saw was not me but that it was just temporary. What I needed to do was speak to who I really am and begin to see me as that. So I applied what I was told day after day and began to speak the word of God over me— Psalm 139:14–18:

> *I will praise You, for I am fearfully and wonderfully made; Marvelous are Your works,*
> *And that my soul knows very well. My frame was not hidden from You,*
> *When I was made in secret, And skillfully wrought in the lowest parts of the earth.*
> *Your eyes saw my substance, being yet unformed. And in Your book they all were written,*
> *The days fashioned for me, When as yet there were none of them.*
> *How precious also are Your thoughts to me, O God! How great is the sum of them!*
> *If I should count them, they would be more in number than the sand;*
> *When I awake, I am still with You.*

I remember my first Sunday back to church I wanted to be in the house of the Lord, to be in the atmosphere of praise and worship with the saints of God. We got to church a little later than usual, but not late, so the parking lot was full. And Jerilyn asked me if I wanted her to let me off at the front entrance, and she would park the car and come and walk in together. But I said no, I would walk with the family together, so we parked and walked. We did our usual, sending the kids on their way and walked into the lobby of the church to make our way inside before praise and worship started.

We were met by one of the ushers, who was also the head of security for the church and a good friend of ours; he looked at me and just stared. He asked, "What is going on with you?" Jerilyn told him that I had been in the hospital for fourteen days diagnosed with bacterial meningitis, and he said to me, "God has a purpose for you, you're not going anywhere." And he helped my wife walk me inside the church to find a seat. The sanctuary was already full, but I knew that if I asked, we could have gone up front, but I was self-conscious and preferred to sit farther back. Besides, the music seemed a little louder than usual and was hurting my ears. We sat down, different ones came over to say hello and to let me know that I was in their prayers; then the music started, and the praise team began to sing, and I almost lost it. The sound was so loud in my ears until I had to put my hands over my ears to try and muffle the sound. There was no pain, just loudness, and I was saying to myself, "I thought that they said I was supposed to be losing my hearing?" Jerilyn bent down to ask me if I wanted to go home, but I said no, I would stay for the word. I made it through the service, and we went home.

Jerilyn: At this point, I was now in full nurturing caretaker mode. Not really knowing what to do but thanking God for having a relationship with him. God's precious Holy Spirit is a constant friend and guide if we are sensitive to him and his guidance. I prayed with every breath I made. I had no clue sometimes what to do next except for the leading of the Holy Spirit. Robert's mood would swing from one mode to another; he was having outburst of anger, and I would wonder where did that came from and why he was responding in this manner. I began to feel like a wounded soldier who had been hit by so many blasts that his nerves were standing on end. As I was walking through this, I began to have flashbacks of my mother being in the hospital and me sharing the load with my aunt of looking after my brothers and sisters. Here it is again, a big load of responsibility. Can someone tell me why all children born first get such a load delegated to them? My brothers and sisters did not want to take instruction from me; they wanted their mother, and so did I. My aunt was stretched to capacity taking care of two families, so I did what I knew to do to alleviate any pressure I could, but there is only so much a seventeen-year-old can do. I began to feel overwhelmed. Now here I was, again caring for a family member; this time it was my husband. The feeling of being overwhelmed is one that can send you places mentally that you really don't want to go. I found myself wanting to be done with all this work and responsibility and asking the Lord to take me to heaven. Then a voice of reason would kick in and say, "What about your husband and children, who will take care of them? You can do this." Can I really? Waves of self-pity would hit me followed by waves of anger. The anger was brimming from the thoughts of "Why me? Why did Robert have to go out and do what he did? Why do I always have to be the responsible one? Why can't everyone else do what they are supposed to do? Lord, when is all of this going to end? I deserve better than this." I don't know if many Christians would be willing to admit their weakness, true weakness in tough situations; it would mean being truly transparent. When we begin walking with the Lord, we are humble and solely dependent on him and seeking his direction continually. When we have walked with the Lord for a while, we sometimes become comfortable and feel like there are things we shouldn't have to experience. Take my thought of "I don't deserve this." Says who? Says me—yes, of course, in my overrated opinion of myself, I didn't deserve it. But when I really examined myself, I began to see, "Yes, you do deserve the con-sequences of your sin. Yes, you do, sistah." What was the sin, not being willing, for one? Willing? Yes, willing to do what was necessary beyond what I knew to become a wife. A wife that Bible describes, not the one I created in my head or developed from information I had received. When we have unrealistic views about any part of who are or who we are supposed to be, we are bound for trouble. I did not know how to be a wife, so I was inept when it came to meet-ing the needs of my husband. Intimacy, sex, respect, and support were a struggle for me. Again, being reared/raised in a single-parent home and, again, having unrealistic views of marriage will shipwreck you. Hearing so many negative things about men growing up caused me to repel my husband once the honeymoon months were over. I judged everything he did by how I would have done it. Even if I didn't say it out loud to him, it created a friction between us because of my thoughts. This friction caused our sex life to be a roller-coaster ride; this led to no intimacy, and finally, respect was at very low ebb. Consequences for our choices do not go away; we do see the results of our bad choices. The reason we serve God is his mercy and grace covers us during these times of walking out of our bad choices. God's loving-kindness is a soothing balm to the wounded soul of a child of God who has stumbled and even fallen. Thank God for his mercy and grace on my life. I am still *here*!

The Worst

The meningitis and the medications I had began to take its toll on my thought processes and emotions; I was still trying to make sense of what had happened to me. One week later, after leaving the hospital, I went in for my follow-up visit with the doctor and to get the test results of the blood that was taken on my last day in the hospital. The doctor came into the room where Jerilyn and I had been waiting; then with all the proper greetings, he asked if he could talk to me alone. Jerilyn left the room, and I asked him what the problem was. Out of nowhere, he asked me if I had ever been with a man sexually; my response made him take a step back. Still weak from the hospital stay and recovering from the meningitis, I gave him a resounding "NO!" and "Why would you ask me something like that?" He proceeded to inform me that the test came back positive for the HIV virus.

"What! Your tests are wrong!" I responded. There was no way that could happen. "Have you had sex with anyone else besides your wife?" "No, I haven't. You're telling me now that I am going to die? I don't think so." He asked if I wanted him to bring my wife in with us. I said yes, and he asked Jerilyn to join us so that she could know what was going on. When she came in, I asked the doctor to tell her what he told me. and he did. After he was finished, I told him that I wanted to be retested, and he asked if Jerilyn wanted to be tested as well, she said yes. We made the appointment for the test and to come back for the results.

Jerilyn: Okay, now here we were again, my head, rocking and reeling. I am trying to figure out is this really happening. Did the doctor just say HIV? How in the world is this possible? We had discussed this; we said we were happy we got married when we did and that we wouldn't have to worry about this deadly disease. This is absolutely crazy. Then my mind took a shift. How could he do this to me, his wife? I mean, what was he thinking, and now he was sitting here lying to the doctor, I could see the lie on his face. The doctor was wondering too how and why he was sticking to this story. I thought I was numb before, now I am numb and in utter, total shock. *Lord, help me! What do I do Lord. This is my husband and we have three children at home and, Lord, we are supposed to be saved Christians, no doubt, and Lord this disease is deadly.*

My mind is racing a mile a minute. I am beyond feeling at this point, I begin to move mechanically and methodically from this moment. Lord, what do I do now? This is so incredibly crazy. I could die, do I want to die? NO! I am only thirty-four years old, too young to die. What about the kids, my family, and all the people that know us—how are they going to be affected by this information/news? People we have gone to church with, people we have shared our faith with and instructed them on how to live saved—what are we going to say behind this? Here we are at ten years of marriage, still working on our marriage, and now we have this on our plate to face.

Robert: Two weeks later, the tests confirmed that we both were HIV positive. I asked the doctor frantically if there was any other way that the disease could be contracted. His response was the virus travels by blood, and the only ways to contract the disease was through sexual contact, blood transfusion, or dirty needles from drug use. In saying that, he asked if either one of us had received a blood transfusion. No. "Do either one of you use drugs in a way that there are needles involved?" No. And the final question: "Have either one of you had sex with anyone else besides your spouse?" *No.*

The Big Lie

I have never cheated on my wife with anyone! That was my immediate response to the doctor's question. The car ride home was one of the quietest we ever had. I don't remember too much more about that afternoon, but that evening, I tossed and turned in bed and could not sleep.

Memories were shooting through my mind, images of people and places. I knew what I had done. I knew I was to blame. I figure leaving Daytona Beach and moving to Orlando would be a fresh start. Like they say about Las Vegas, what happens in Vegas stays in Vegas. Not so! Unrepented sin leaves a scent. *Numbers 32:23 "But if ye will not do so, behold, ye have sinned against the LORD: and be sure your sin will find you out."*

It was about 1:30 a.m., I sat up, with tears in my eyes and fear ruling my heart, getting ready to pack my bags and leave. Just then, Jerilyn woke up; she came around the bed and sat next to me and asked me what was going on.

How do I begin to tell the mother of my children, the woman that I stood up and vowed before God and others that I would "stay true to her until death do us part" I have given her the HIV virus? Time stood still at that moment as I began to confess everything that I had ever done that brought us to this crossroads in our lives and our relationship. Told her that I had cheated on her, and because of that sin, I have given her one of the world's deadliest disease for which there is no cure. I told her that I was going to pack my clothes and leave. She had all the help that she would need with her family and friends, and they would make sure that she would be okay. I would just disappear, and she would never hear from me again.

Jerilyn: How I arrived at the responses that came out of my mouth I will never know. It had to be God, because my mind was arguing with almost every word that was coming out of my mouth. My mouth was saying, "Oh, it's okay Robert. I understand, we can work this out." My mind was saying, *How in the world you could do this to me and these children?* My mouth was saying, "We are married, and we said for better or for worse, you don't have to leave." But, my mind was saying, *You are right, you need to leave. You are the one who broke the vows and sat in the doctor's office and lied to my face several times about it, how dare you.* Although my mind had arguments, because of the fact I had shifted into mechanical/methodical mode, my spirit was able to lead me. If my mind had led me during this critical moment, who knows what the end result would have been. Divorce?!

Robert: What do you say? There aren't any comforting words that would be good enough to answer to this. King David sinned against God by taking the wife of Uriah, Bathsheba, then getting her pregnant and trying to hide it by trying to send Uriah home to his wife after he had just come home from a battle. But instead, Uriah slept at the door of the king's house with the other servants. So David had to come up with another plan, and took it to the next step and had him sent to the front line of the battle, had his men to withdraw from Uriah, and he was killed. No more problem, right? Wrong. God knows everything about us: where we've been, what we do, how we do it, and who we do it with, "be sure, your sin will find you out" (Numbers 32:23). I begged for her forgiveness, and she said she did. But why would she do that? How could she do that? She would never look at or think of me in the same way again. *God, our lives are in your hands.*

Broken Vows

I wasn't supposed to be here! This was not the way it was supposed to be! I broke my marriage vows. This was not in my life's plan. I saw the pain that the sin of adultery caused my mother, the betrayal, the cover-ups by the church and family members, and the effects that it had on our entire family, even as sons. But how did I get here?

Secrets, unconfessed sin! It didn't start after I got married; it overflowed into the marriage from my singlehood. There were sexual areas in my life that I thought for sure would end after I got married. I thought that I would not have to deal with or want to watch pornography anymore or even think about another woman in a sexual way, besides my wife. I mean, I have a wife now, and I could have all the sex I wanted. I would not need to go outside of my house to look for anything. *Not so!* Though I was in church, at the time, surrounded by friends, even reading and studying the Bible, full of the Holy Ghost, praise and worship leader, minister/elder, and still there was sin in my life that I did not deal with that carried over into my marriage. Unconfessed sin! It was me that made these vows, not my father. I can't blame this all on my upbringing, and I had a choice. Ezekiel 18:1:

> The word of the LORD came unto me again, saying, "What mean ye, that ye use this proverb concerning the land of Israel, saying, The fathers have eaten sour grapes, and the children's teeth are set on edge?

As I live, saith the Lord GOD, ye shall not have occasion any more to use this proverb in Israel. Behold, all souls are mine; as the soul of the father, so also the soul of the son is mine: the soul that sinneth, it shall die."

I sinned against God.

Men were created as visual beings. We were created to see and identify and put a name to the things around us; "we call it like we see it," but we were supposed to see everything through the eyes of God and less through eyes of the flesh. That's why it is so important that we, as men, be so mindful of what we allow through our eye gates. I didn't learn that until it was too late. As young men, we weren't taught not to look at the red fruit; we were taught, "if it looks good, take and eat," if the truth be told. Job said it best in chapter 31 verse 1, *"I made a covenant with my eyes not to look lustfully at a young woman." (NIV)*

Exposure to pornography at a very young age, as well as being molested by a close friend of the family's son, both of which no one knew about was the beginning of—*secrets!* Once those images are burned into your mind and memory bank, it takes the power of God by His Spirit to deliver you from it. There is a spirit of lust that attaches itself to pornography, and lust is insatiable. It needs to feed, and the more you feed it, the more it wants. I've been in places and around people that I never ever thought that I would be or should have been, just to satisfy the appetite of that lustful spirit and the flesh. And it didn't help my cause at all that I had such low self-esteem and having a bad outlook of myself, which caused me to withdraw from everyone around me and spend a lot of time alone with my thoughts. That is where the enemy (the devil) wants you. Those feelings of inadequacy, depression, and loneliness lead you into whatever someone gives you or you give into so easily: the deceptions of what you think of or what looks like caring and love. Anything that will make you feel like you are something besides trash. But you would think that marrying a beautiful young lady, someone who would dare to be seen with you, all that would go away—*it doesn't!*

Single-Parent Home

(Jerilyn)

I had a part to play in all this as well. I was raised in a single-parent home with a mother, who was in the driver's seat as well as me being the eldest of her five children; it put me in a pseudo parental role. These things set me up to be a woman who was not real submissive or used to meeting the needs of a man.

Now, let's be brutally honest here. I did not know how to, nor did I have a desire to meet those needs in reality. Now mind you, I had an image in my head of what I wanted my marriage to be like. I had spent lots of time watching all the Christian couples in church, gleaning ideas to put into my dream ideas of what marriage should be like. and I armed myself with the scripture Proverbs 31:10–31.

None of this said to me that I would have any real challenges in my marriage. *Not!* As I mentioned earlier, I was still struggling with the process of becoming *one* in a marriage, something that we all go through. This makes me reflect on a wonderful piece of advice a wise brother in Christ gave us, he said, "Always remember this as you are about to get married: here are two single people who have been single for twenty-plus years separately, now they are coming together and trying to undo forty-plus years of singlehood to become *one* flesh." This was an excellent piece of advice. Now, how do you really implement this? This is why we must be counseled before marriage and after.

I got married right out of my mother's house, and I was so *green* about many things of what real life was and to be newly married, that was a concoction for disaster. Well, here is the disaster: we both have HIV. Two becoming one, missing steps, trying to bring our flesh under subjection to what the word of God says is a Godly marriage. I really didn't understand the needs of a man, and especially not one with a broken spirit. From the outside looking in, I didn't know how to be a married woman. Single-parent homes produce strong mature children, but they miss out on the day to day of seeing a man and woman interacting in marriage. In these homes, based on my experience, the children miss out on some valuable lessons that come from seeing Godly parents live together in daily life. Working together in various situations, such as no money to pay bills, car(s) in need of repair, a child in rebellion and misguidance by those in church leadership, praying together about the problems of life, and just loving one another no matter what.

These are the challenges our marriages face every day, but instead of one person trying to juggle it all, God called two. Someone has to talk about it, truthfully and without being super spiritual but sticking to biblical principles. This story is a real-life testimony of pain and hurt in marriage by a real-life couple.

Even with what seemingly is a death sentence looming over the union, it is possible to live. Psalm 118:17: "I shall not die, but live to declare the works of the Lord."

Neither of us remembers how this scripture was presented to us, but once it was, we began to declare it over our lives. And here we are, living witnesses to tell the story.

Men, the Glory of God

As men, we are created by God, in His image. We are visionaries/dreamers/innovators, we are protectors/defenders, we are husbands, we are fathers, we are leaders, we are pioneers, and we are the glory of God (1 Corinthians 11:7: "For a man indeed ought not to cover his head, forasmuch as he is the image and glory of God"). But men are also fallen; we're prideful, arrogant; our "hearts are deceitful and desperately wicked" (Jeremiah 17:9); we lovers of themselves, greedy, adulterers, idolaters—shall I go on? But "what is man that Thou art mindful of him and the son of man that You should visit him" (Psalm 8:4). "Lord, what is man, that you take knowledge of him? Or the son of man, that You are mindful of him?" (Psalm 144:3) "What is man, that You should exalt him, that You should set Your Heart on him that You should visit or attend to him every morning and test him every moment?" (Job 7:17 and 18)

God loves man, for better or for worse. It does not mean that He agrees with the bad decision making that we do or the sins that we commit over and over again, but He's always standing there, waiting for us to come back home to where we belong.

We spend so much of our lives searching for our identity in this world, until we forget who we really are. Face it: we were created in the image of God that is our DNA, which is what defines us, but we fight so hard to be just the opposite because we don't feel that that's good enough. We have chased a fantasy all this time, and it's cost us, dearly. It has cost us time, relationship after relationship, our families, and our children. We have been chasing the wrong roots, believing that will identify us. *Not so.*

What are we looking for? What is it that we think is missing from our life that drives us into the directions we choose?

If God wrote my story because He is the author and the finisher of my faith and He knew me before I was formed in my mother's womb and He knows the thoughts and plan for my life. If this is so, why don't I ask Him to read me a story, my story, my life, my purpose, my destiny, and follow it?

Generation after generation of young men drive themselves to be better than their fathers, driven by that inner pride that says, "I can do better, go farther, and have more." What happened to that little boy who once looked up at his daddy with such admiration and longing to be just like him? He saw strength, he saw pride in a good honest day's work, and he saw how daddy loved his wife and how he treated her. I always hear people talk about or use the phrase "daddy's little girl," but what about "daddy's little boy" or "daddy's boy" instead of "momma's boy"? There are so many sons out there still in search of that daddy that went missing so many years ago, searching for time lost, searching for their identity. We have allowed our hearts to be infected with instability and wanderlusts.

We are raised not to show what people may think of as weakness or softness. "We can't cry, we're men." "Keep your emotions in check." "Don't let them see you as sweet." So we shut everything in and hide our true selves. If you always show strength, you will never know how to deal with your weaknesses. It's okay to be read of men. That's how you know that you are flawed. Someone from the outside seeing the real you, those hidden things that you don't want anyone to see.

I am neither a psychiatrist nor a psychologist. I am a man, flawed just like you, who spent a lot of time searching for something that I thought was lost, but it was right there all the time. You see, when you fall into the trap of insecurity, anything that seems like or anyone that shows you any type of love and attention will draw you right into it or them very easily. It's an open door for the enemy to come in and steal, kill, and destroy your purpose. I have lived it. Though you are married to a wonderful person who loves you for who you are, if there should come any time of feeling rejection or lack of love or affection, you go out looking for comfort. It's a deception. What you think is an oasis in the dessert is really a mirage; your eyes, mind, and heart have deceived you. It's all a distraction, a ploy to get you off course so that you will not fulfill your destiny or call on your life.

Relationship

I was sitting one day watching a little TV, one of my favorite cop shows, and there was a very interesting scenario going on. On his day off, one of the investigators was watching his neighbor's son while she was on her way to work. He took the boy outside to ride his bike on the sidewalk when down the street from them; a convenience store was being robbed with men carrying guns. He told the boy to ride his bike home and the chase was on. He announced himself as a police officer, and the gunman began to fire at him. He chased the gunman, but he got away. Coming back to the scene of the crime, he noticed a crowd of people gathering together. And as he approached, he was shocked to see lying there on the ground was the body of the young boy he had sent home, he had been struck and killed by a stray bullet from the gunfight with the robbers. The investigator took the boy's death very hard and had become very distant as well as doing everything he could to support the boy's mother. In the meantime, while taking care of the needs of and comforting his neighbor, he forgot the anniversary of the relationship between him and his girlfriend, who was also his coworker, and that led to problems within the relationship. All his emotional and moral support was coming from the boy's mother as well as pouring out everything to her. Was his girlfriend angry, *yes*! But the real cause of her anger was not that he forgot their anniversary but the feeling that he did not trust her enough to lean on her through his grieving or emotional process. To her, it was not just a girlfriend-boyfriend relationship, but an emotional life-changing relationship. Now, what she didn't know and found out later was that he and the young boy's mother had fallen into a comforting or co-dependent relationship that had become sexual. Boy, sometimes we men can be soooo stupid! We are tossed and driven by what we think is the most important member of our body. The person that he should have gone to for comfort and help, he pushed away. In doing so, driven by guilt over what happened to the young boy, he fell into the arms of a grieving single mother who needed comforting more than he did.

Now, at the end of the story, he loses everything. His neighbor, the boy's mother, realizes what was going on is all about guilt and not real love then cuts the relationship off. Then he turns back to his girlfriend for comfort, but she knows that things were not right and asked him flat out about the relationship with the other woman. He admitted what had happened, and he lost her as well.

We men fall into the same situation all the time; we love to try and fix things, especially if we are the ones that broke it, whether by accident or on purpose. I know, ladies, you say, "Not my husband." Well—yes, he does. But the thing is, all men don't fix things in the same way, especially if they don't know how to and will feel pressured to act rather than respond to any given need.

Ephesians 5:25–33 (KJV):

> *Husbands, love your wives, even as Christ also loved the church, and gave himself for it; that he might sanctify and cleanse it with the washing of water by the word, that he might present it to himself a glorious church, not having spot, or wrinkle, or any such thing; but that it should be holy and without blemish. So ought men to love their wives as their own bodies. He that loves his wife loves himself. For no man ever yet hated his own flesh; but nourishes and cherishes it, even as the Lord the church: For we are members of his body, of his flesh, and of his bones. For this cause shall a man leave his father and mother, and shall be joined unto his wife, and*

they two shall be one flesh. This is a great mystery: but I speak concerning Christ and the church. Nevertheless let every one of you in particular so love his wife even as himself; and the wife see that she reverence her husband.

This scripture is far from the domineering way wives have been and are treated today, in the "twenty-first" century and in times past. We men are called—*yes, called*—to love our wives as Christ Loves the church and *gave* Himself for it, not to be dictators or to have dominion over them. That was meant for the earth and all the living things that fly, creep, or swim, not of our wives. How did and does Jesus show this love for the church? He gave up everything for us so that we may be saved, even knowing the condition we were in. Our first assignment as husbands starts at the beginning—Genesis 2:24: "Therefore shall a man leave his father and mother and shall cleave to his wife; and they shall be one flesh." We husbands are commanded by God to leave, cleave, and to be one flesh. The problem is, we aren't doing any leaving or cleaving which helps us to be one flesh.

Now What?

This was the beginning of the test of my life. How was I going to live out what had come out of my mouth from the spirit? My soul was still struggling with many things and still learning to be married—you know, the becoming *one* process. Now here is this wrench being thrown into the engine of my life. You ask why share all this in a book, our personal life? The truth of life is not being shared. *Transparency* is another word that has become a catchphrase in Christianity. Is anyone really being transparent?

This book is our life, transparent for the world to see.

Robert: Our lives would forever change and by no means would be the same from that night until now. We asked the doctor where we needed to go from here, is there medication we needed to start taking. He told us that our immune systems were currently strong and our CD4 and T-Cell numbers were high and that there was no need for us to take any meds at this point, that there were many people who lived all their lives without taking any, but his strong advice was that we get the medications. Exercise and a change of diet would also be very advantageous to us. So, that's what we did. We didn't tell anyone anything about our condition. For all people knew, I was still recovering from the meningitis, which in itself, took a big toll on me physically and mentally. We put ourselves on a vitamin regimen; I started walking, changed the way I purchased food and prepared it. Though we were doing all these things and doing very well, still, there was the HIV that I had brought into my home. I started doing a study on this disease to find out how it worked and how it was going to affect us physically. Some of the information was encouraging, but there were others that were not.

I knelt down in my room next to my bed and talked to God about all of it, not that He didn't know everything already. I prayed, "Lord, I brought this in my house and to my wife. If anyone should suffer, it should be me. I will take whatever comes with this sin. Don't let Jerilyn suffer in any way, she has done nothing wrong. She already has to look at the man who did this thing to her. *Please*, I will take it."

I had no idea what was about to happen to me.

Jerilyn: I had no idea Robert was praying like this. I had sent up many prayers myself. Prayers like, "God help me, and I don't want to die. Lord, how do I live with this man now? Lord, the children, will I see them grow up? Lord, what do I do now? Lord help me to stay here in my marriage. Lord, I have waves of anger just washing over me every time I think about this situation we are in. How in the world did we get here, what did I do to deserve this?"

Let's be honest here, we all begin to say this. We all really believe deep down inside that we are doing the right thing all the time after we get saved. What a deception! This deception is perpetuated because we as Christians have developed a sin meter. You know this Sin is greater and worse than this Sin over here. *Not so!* Sin is sin. Growing up as the eldest child always places a greater demand on you. So here is this eldest child who had her feet held to the fire almost daily, feeling like why do I deserve this? I did what my elders told me to do and didn't really cause my mother any real trouble, you know, like a teen pregnancy, bad grades in school and bad-influence friends directing my life. So my life has been good. But the word of God says, "All have sinned and come short of the Glory of God." So this deception that if my sin is not as bad as the next Christian makes me better or good is not scriptural. So my thinking was warped, concerning my life with this new news. Robert had gone out and brought this disease into our marriage, why do I have to suffer? Yes, Christians have negative inappropriate thoughts and need adjustments in the word daily to counteract them. How dare I think that Robert deserved worse than me because I had been "good" all my life? Again, I say *not so* this is a *huge* deception. Now to find out that Robert is praying as he is just solidifies the error. Yes, there are consequences to our sins, but we should not ask God for things that are contrary to his word.

Wages

The marriage vows that we stand and commit to have two things they have in common, they all take *unconditional love* and *unfeigned faith*. And you definitely need to have them both when the real bad times come. If you don't, your marriage will become a casualty of war, and you will be left disillusioned and sometimes bitter. "For better and worst; for richer, for poorer; in sickness and in health—until death do us part."

These words were put to the test more when we moved to Jonesboro, Georgia, in 2004. This is why you really need to know—*no*, you better know who you are marrying and who you are married to.

Let me explain:

After a year or so following the whole ordeal with the meningitis and the news of the HIV, we were trying desperately to get on with our lives. Jerilyn was still employed for the company where she worked and I was looking for work having been released from my position as the head chef of a local restaurant that had fallen into financial difficulty. We were actually doing pretty well despite not having a job, but I had lined up what appeared to be a good prospect with another restaurant chain nearby. But I, figuring that maybe we could get a new start somewhere else, decided to take my younger brother, Cleveland, up on his offer for us to move to Georgia, which wasn't a good move in hindsight because my wife was not in total agreement with it. Now listen to me, brothers, Please. Sometimes, the greatest mistake that we make is not to listen to the "help mate" the Lord has blessed us with. Sometimes we need to be still and allow God to work in us his will. See, I was still running from my past, but at the cost of my family.

Amos 3:3: "Can two walk together, except they be agreed?"

We still hadn't told anyone of our diagnosis or what condition we were in. No one at church, neither one of our families or friends, our jobs, nor our children—only Jerilyn and I knew what was going on with us. We had made a decision to step out in faith and believe God for healing for the both of us, not only for the disease we were fighting but our marriage as well.

It was the summer of July 2003 when I loaded up the back of a U-Haul truck, packed up my family in the car that we had, and drove north from Orlando, Florida, to Riverdale, Georgia, where my brother and his family lived. He and I had discussed me helping him to finish his basement so that we could move in with him and his family. I had sent money ahead of time for him to use for that reason so that we would have a private place for my family to live during our transition. We arrived in the city early enough so that we could get the kids settled in and registered for school then began looking for work for Jerilyn and me. It was good to see my brother after so many years of being apart; it was like we had to get to know each other all over again, seeing that I had moved away from my hometown after my mother died—so did he, but he just moved a little farther than I did. After about two months, I had a found a position at a restaurant at the very top area of Atlanta that soon proved to be too far away for the commute. So I was able to find another position closer to where my brother lived, and I worked both until my two weeks' notice was up on the first one. The second job came with pretty good benefits for me and my family, so I began to set up doctor's appointments for me and Jerilyn to get ourselves checked out.

In the meantime, Jerilyn was able to land a position for herself as an administrative assistant for the American Heart Association. When we got our first paychecks, we opened an account at a local bank near us and soon began putting money away and started looking for our own place. Things started to get a little tight at Cleveland's house, if you know what I mean, and I think that we really just wanted our own space in addition to more privacy. It was at that time Jerilyn and I decided to get our own apartment for our family so we moved to Jonesboro, just a few minutes away from my brother, It put us both closer to our jobs, and the kids were able to attend school just across the street from where the complex sat. It was fairly new apartment with three bedrooms, two baths on the third floor of the building. It had a small living room/dining room combo with a nice open kitchen and a small screened in patio that overlooked the woods in back of the complex. The complex also had a nice playground for the kids to play, which there were a lot of them, and a large parking lot where I taught them to ride their bicycles. It was a wonderful time for all of us. The church we attended was about thirty to forty-five minutes from us, where we attended regularly, and our children really enjoyed the children's ministry there. I had not seen them that excited in a while; things were good. By December, the position that I thought would be the one closed down for lack of business, and I was looking for another job. But the Lord granted me favor, and I finally landed a steady position in January of 2004, for a very popular restaurant chain that was opening a new store in Camp Creek, Georgia. area. I must say, it was a pretty smooth transition; we didn't skip a beat.

Opening a brand-new restaurant takes a lot of work, energy, and time. I got in on the ground floor of it all as they were finishing it up the final details of the building; we were in an intense training program learning the standardized recipes and company policies and procedures. The hours were long and hard; at first, we were on a rotating schedule until we officially opened the doors. After that, it was on. I was literally working seven days a week and twelve sometimes more hours a day for weeks on end. Jerilyn would drop me of to work every morning at five thirty and picked me up around six o' clock at night. The kids would always come with her as they were still too young to leave home by themselves. At times, I would take them over to this little Chinese restaurant behind ours and treat them to dinner; they loved it. I worked like this for about three months straight. The money was good, but I never saw it because I was working most of the time. Jerilyn took care of everything. I gave her the paycheck, and she did her thing—life was pretty good. But the long hours and no day off started to take a toll on my body. I would get home, shower and eat, if I felt like it, then stay up as long as I could just to spend some time with my wife and children before they had to go to bed. That gave me just enough time to settle down so that I could sleep myself and then get up early the next morning to start it all over again.

Then it happened, April 21, 2004—everything came crashing down. I woke up that morning not feeling too hot, I thought that maybe I was just tired from all of the hours that I had been working, but it turned out to be the beginning of four years straight of me going in and out of the hospital.

I got to work that morning as usual. It was a pretty cold day, and as I started to work, I started feeling very weak. Now I consider myself to be a pretty strong guy, so I sucked it up and tried to continue to work, but it just wasn't happening. I got extremely dizzy, and my knees started to buckle, so I grabbed hold of the edge of the three-compartment sink where I had been working to prevent myself from falling on my butt. My co-workers around me started to ask if I was okay. I told them that I needed to go home and one of them said, "You need to go and say something to one of the managers." I staggered out to the dining room area where the managers were having a meeting and asked the shift manager if I could speak with him. He came over to me and asked, "What was going on?" I told him how I was feeling, and he suggested that I sit down for a few minutes to see if I would feel better. I did as he said and sat down on one of the wooden benches out front. I can't really explain what was going on with me, but I felt like I was coming apart. I couldn't get my thoughts together, and my breathing was labored. At that point, I couldn't take any more, I felt like I would pass out any minute. So, I told the manager that I needed to go and that I was going to call my brother Cleveland to pick me up because Jerilyn had the car. I could barely walk. Some of the guys from the kitchen came out to help me to the other side of the restaurant so that when my brother got there, I wouldn't have far to walk. I don't know how long it took

Cleveland to get there; it seemed like an eternity, but I looked up and saw him coming through the door. I tried to explain to him what was going on, but I was so weak. He helped me up. I had no strength in my legs, the other guys grabbed me and helped me to the car, and we headed to the nearest hospital. Cleveland called his wife Lisa, then she got a hold of Jerilyn, and they met us there.

As soon as we arrived, Cleveland pulled up close to the entrance of the ER, parked, and ran inside to get a wheelchair for me. I was still very weak, and my breathing wasn't getting any better. We checked in, and the nurse told us to have a seat in the waiting area and some-one would be with us momentarily. While we were waiting, Jerilyn and Lisa showed up. Jerilyn immediately came over and stood next to me to get a feel of how I was doing by rubbing my back and ask-ing if they had said anything yet. We sat there for what seemed like an eternity before I asked Jerilyn to call my doctor. She got in touch with him, and he asked that I be brought to his office.

Stop! Now, I need to take the time to explain that I had been seeing this doctor for more than three months with him checking me for everything that ailed me, but I still had not told him about my HIV status. Even when I would have fever spikes, when I would catch colds frequently and could not function with my everyday life, he would ask me repeatedly if there was anything that he needed to know concerning my health. I would not tell him after all, I was calling those things that be not as they were just like the Bible said—right? Wrong! I had been holding back the truth about my HIV sta-tus, honestly believing that I was standing on my faith that God would heal me and that no one would ever have to know anything about it. I honestly believed that what I was doing was an act of faith, but it turned out that it was more presumption than faith. After all, I had watched a preacher on television who said that God had healed him of cancer. He said that when he was first diagnosed, he did not tell anybody but his wife. He went on to say that he closed himself off in a room of his house with his Bible and began to read every scripture in it that talked about healing and began to speak the words to his body and believe God for healing. The next thing I know, I see him telling his testimony that he had gone back to the doctor and found that the cancer was no longer there; he was healed. When I heard that I said, "God, if you can do that for him, you can do it for me." But what I did not understand at that time in my life was that everything that happens for someone else may not happen for you. There are things that God allows each of us to go through because He knows what each of us can and cannot handle or bear.

"Wherefore let him that thinketh he standeth take heed lest he fall. There hath no temptation taken you but such as is common to man: but God *is* faithful, who will not suffer you to be tempted above that ye are able; but will with the temptation also make a way to escape, that ye may be able to bear *it*" (1 Corinthians 10:12, 13).

My mistake was not to be truthful up front with my doctor so that he could assess what kind of condition I was in from the beginning, that if I had been forthcoming in advance, maybe the things that were about to happen with me and my family would not have.

Now back to that day. My brother and sister-in-law went home to watch or children while Jerilyn drove me to the doctor's office. Upon arriving, Jerilyn did the best she could to help me into the office as I was still very week. I was bundled in a big brown winter coat, laying on the examining bed shivering, curled up in a ball not seeming able to control myself. The doctor came in as I lay there and said to me "Mr. Ward, I don't know what is going on with you, are you sure you've told me everything about your health?" It was at this point that I made my confession and told him of my HIV status. I could see the angry and frustrated expression on his face as he voiced "you should have let me know that from the beginning, that's a whole different way of treating you"! He then walked out and came back in within a few minutes to let me know he had the name of an Infectious Disease doctor that he wanted me to see. In the meantime, he prescribed me some medication to break the fever then made an appointment for me with the Specialist. But, between that visit and the other with the new doctor, I hit rock bottom. One day, while alone in our apartment, my wife was at work and the children were in school after eating breakfast I felt something wrong. I ran to the bathroom and seemed like losing everything, my chest ached, couldn't catch my breath. I sat there in the bathroom feeling like I was about to die. I called 911, told them what was going on and they told to stay calm, they were on their way. After giving them my address and hanging up from them, I called Jerilyn to let her know what was going on, she immediately left work heading my way. I was so weak and felt like I couldn't move but within me, I heard myself begin to pray "Lord, please don't let me die like this! Not like! I cleaned myself up and headed to the living room to wait for whomever got there first. There was a knock on the door, the paramedics had arrived. They immediately began to do what they do, taking vitals and asking questions about my condition. At that point Jerilyn walked in as they were strapping me to the gurney for the long trip down three flights of stairs. Their main concern was my blood pressure as it was extremely high and my breathing was much labored. Now imagine having to take a man, 6'3" tall and 325lbs down those amount of steep stairs on a standard size gurney, it was going to happen. So they walked me down until we got to the bottom, then had me lay on the gurney. My wife was still upstairs gathering somethings as the loaded me in the ambulance. I remember, as they were closing the door's, I saw my brother and my father standing there watching. I thought I was dreaming. I was admitted to the hospital and diagnosed with PCP pneumonia (Pneumocystis pneumonia), it is a life threatening lung infection that can affect people with weakened immune systems, such as those infected with HIV.

My father had flown in driven up from South Florida to see he and my brother had just gotten there to surprise me as they were loading me into the ambulance to take me to the hospital. He would come into my room, pray, and talk to me every day for about three days then he had to get back as he was a pastor of a local church down South. But even he believed that I was going to die. They believed that I had committed the unpardonable sin against God and that "the wages of sin is death."

You see, HIV/AIDS has a stigma, especially for men. The first thing people think is, "He must have been in some type of homosexual relationship" or "You were on the DL" (down low). Ignorance is not bliss.

It was after I had been in there for a couple of days that a nurse practitioner came into my room, sat next to my bed, and asked me if I knew what was going on with me. I told her no, and she proceeded to tell me that I had full-blown AIDS. She told me that my CD4 counts were too low, less than 20, and they were trying to get them to come up with the medications they were giving me intravenously, but it didn't look good. I asked her if she was a Christian; she said no. I told her that I was and God was going to heal me and that I would be fine. She smiled at me and said, "I will be in touch with you once you leave the hospital, if you need anything, give me a call." Then she left and I never saw her again. They were not expecting me to leave that hospital. The doctors sent people in, over the next few days, to talk with me about communities where people with the AIDS virus would go and live out their time with others with the same condition. It was like an apartment complex where they could live and be taken care of by nurses and doctors. They wouldn't come right out and say it, but I knew that the people they were referring to were not expected to live long lives. But why were they saying these things to me? I had a wife and three children to take care of, and I have a life to live.

Family members had already gone to Jerilyn and told her to prepare for a funeral because I was not going to live. That is why you need to know the word for yourself and guard your ears, eyes, and heart when the worst times come. I remember that last night in the hospital so vividly. After everyone had left, it was late, and I could not sleep. I looked up at the light over my bed, and I began to talk to God. "Lord, is this it? Is this how my life ends? What about the dreams and visions you've shown me concerning my life, family and ministry? Is it all over?" As I lay there, it seemed as though a picture screen opened up before me, and I could see myself preaching from a stage behind a podium, dressed in a dark-colored suit, and there were hundreds of people sitting there, listening to me. I could see my wife sitting in the front row to my right smiling at me. This vision continued on throughout the night. Scene after scene flashed on my consciousness so vivid was each scene. It was about 3:30 or 4:00 a.m. when the nurse came in to check my vitals that I finally went to sleep.

Saturday afternoon, I was released from the hospital and went home. I could barely eat because of the mouth sores. I had to sip soup through a straw, and I would cry and shake with each attempt as my children watched. I barely slept because of the nightmares I was having because of the medications I was taking. I would wake up the same time every night choking on my own vomit and having to run to the bathroom to clear my throat. I still had temperature spikes that left me shaking uncontrollably, and my daughter Brea, having to get cold ice towels to put on my head and on my chest to help bring the fevers down. She was my helper while Jerilyn was at work. I would show up to doctors' appointments, check in only for them to be surprised that I was there. I actually could hear the nurse go back and tell the doctor that I was there and hear the tone and reaction in his voice—one of shock, "He's here?!"

Proverbs 18:14 says, *The spirit of a man will sustain him in sickness, but who can bear a broken spirit?*"

I have been in and out of the hospital since that time and have endured a lot of pain that I don't wish on anybody, but God has blessed and healed my body in every case. I could very easily say that I must not be in faith or have enough faith for God to heal me totally, and there may be people who say that God will not heal me because they think that HIV/AIDS is an unpardonable sin. I say to them, "Where were you when God created the worlds and brought light into existence?" I am a child of God, and I know he loves me and that no one can take that away. His Grace is sufficient for me. I have a wife who had every right to leave me for dead and to divorce me and go on with her own life, and I believe God would have blessed her and my children, but the Love of God is too deep and too wide for natural man to comprehend it. But for those that do comprehend God's love, they help to change the very course of life and break the backbone of Satan himself.

Family Response

Jerilyn: Robert and I now knew we must share this information with our families. They need to know so that in the event that something happens to either of us, our children would be provided for. This is what you call a reality check. We had kept this all a secret for many reasons. One reason is the stigma attached to the disease. Secondly, when people get involved in your life, they bring more to what you already have to maintain. And finally, because of some teaching we had received in a church we attended, that you just don't share everything about your life with everyone. We felt like if we began to share with everyone, then there would be negative words and actions we would have to deal with. But there is no way to avoid that; it is a part of life even if you are doing what is right. So Robert told his family, and I told mine. There was outrage and anger from both sides for various reasons. Like "What is wrong with you why didn't you tell us? Man, what were you thinking, are you on the DL (downlow)?" "Girl, you need to leave him. Why would you spend time with us this close and not let us know what you are carrying you could have affected us?" I received more talk than Robert as I proceeded to tell my friends too. I don't know what made me subject myself to the barrage of words that came. I didn't not stop them from saying the things they said to me. I guess because I knew already what their reactions would be. I know now that is why we had kept it a secret for this long. It is now 2004, and we have been living with the disease for exactly two years when we began to tell our family. We were already pretty much isolated just going to church and hearing the word and spending some time with family and friends. But now, the information about our health has been revealed. We did spend some time with family and friends, but very little. The ones we spent time with knew of our condition but did not let that stop them from reaching out to us. But we knew there was speculation, anger, outrage, and even some fear growing for both of us. We knew that anger was building toward Robert because he had brought the disease into our lives. Speculation was growing as they were wondering how, when, and why he would do what he did. We knew that for me, folks were wondering what was wrong with me. "He did that to you, girl, you need to leave." I received all kinds of advice during these early days of revealing our condition. Some of the advice was sound, and the rest had to be discarded. Family members stayed in contact with us real good over the next four years, asking about our health, but staying their distance as we expected would happen. But after year four there was no more conversation regarding our condition; no one really asked except a close few who were watching the hand of God work in our lives. Needless to say, this makes for a very lonely walk. Our greatest concerns were our children. We talked at length about them and how this was going to affect them. We had also talked at length when we first got married, deciding not to keep secrets in our family unit. We had been recipients of secrets in family. Secrets kill families. Secrets created unnecessary family breeches. Secrets have been the cause of many deaths. We had shared everything we could think of with each other about our past and where we had been and what we had done with each other. Now it was time to talk to our children. Nicholas, Brea, and Jessica were still pretty young at this point. One still in elementary school, the other two in middle school; but because we had opened the information up to family, we knew that they would eventually hear someone say something. We did not want them to hear it from anyone else and to get the wrong attitude when it was presented to them. We did not want them to hear whispers about their parents from kids at school or adults in conversation as they saw them walk by talking. So at ages thirteen, twelve, and eleven, we sat our children down and told them about our condition and what it meant. This initial conversation was not real detailed but enough so that they were aware of what was going on. We had subsequent conversations with them so that by the time they we all in high school they have full knowledge and understanding of what was happening in our lives. This was not an easy task, but to avoid misunderstandings and detrimental secrets of the family proportion, we told them. Their responses to us remained the same, and are to this day: "You are our parents, and we love you."

Conclusion

(Robert)

Let's just stop for a moment. While you are sitting there, wherever you are, and if you are married, let me ask a question. Can you remember the worst time(s) in your marriage? I mean, that time when all hell broke loose in your relationship, the pain it caused, all the hurt, and the feelings of betrayal, whatever it may have been? What did you do? Don't rush this question or try to make it seem like you held it all together; be real for a minute. The person you vowed, in front of witnesses, that you were going to spend the rest of your life with just told you the worst thing that you could ever imagine. What was your reaction?

The response that I received from my wife, Jerilyn, was not the one that I was expecting. It did not matter to me, nor was I concerned about anybody else's response but Jerilyn's. Family didn't matter, in-laws didn't matter, as I didn't commit to them. She had every right to leave me, whether by law and by scripture, but she didn't. Why? Because I'm so great—no, she had more in her than I had in me, that God kinda love. You may not have gotten that response from your spouse. Maybe your spouse doesn't know, or you both know but have shut yourselves off from the world. Or maybe your decision was to leave and get a divorce. Sooner or later, you will have to come to terms with it, good or bad. And you can try, but there is no way, if you have any decency or any truth in you whatsoever, to justify committing adultery. Sir/ma'am, there is nothing that you can do or say that can justify you cheating on your spouse, not before God—and that's who you will have to answer to on that day. But we do try, don't we? "He doesn't treat me like he used to." "She doesn't understand my needs." "He just doesn't listen to me." Or this is a good one, "I've fallen out of love with him/her."

Adultery is a sin, just like fornication; or for you who don't know, "premarital sex" is sin, and there is a wage to be paid for sin, death (Romans 6:23). HIV/AIDS is a wage. STDs are wages. Divorce is a wage, etc. My relationship with my wife died. Trust died! Because of the way the disease went through my body, I could not work, and the thing that I loved to do so much I could not stand long enough to do. I was in and out of hospitals and taking all types of medications. We literally had to start all over again. Wages. We really do think, as Christians, that there are no wages or consequences for our sins, we do. But the thing is, we have an advocate or an intercessor (Jesus Christ) who is forever making intercession on our behalf before the Father God. Hebrews 7:25; *"Wherefore he is able also to save them to the uttermost that come unto God by him, seeing he ever liveth to make intercession for them."* You may be where I was, in the same situation, and have not said anything to your wife or anybody. Now is the time to set things right. You don't have to do it alone. If you have a pastor, someone you know that you can trust, go to them. Tell them what you have done and could they help you tell your spouse, even if they go with you, anything but just letting it go on.

Jerilyn: Is this real? Some of you may ask or wonder. Yes, this is a real-life experience with real people, staying together through one of the biggest challenges of their lives. February 2012 will be ten years since the beginning of what seemed to be a lose-lose situation. Why write about our personal experience and open up our lives for all to see? Because there are lives that can be changed and altered forever for the good by reading this testimony.

How are you doing this? This is a question that sends me to my core value system. I made a choice. I really did not know what the end result would be for this choice, but it has been a journey. When you are on a journey, you understand that there is a destination. My destination is God's full and complete promise in my life fulfilled. Aside from this journey, I just want to live. No one ever sets their life out to *die*. When I chose to stay with my husband, I did not know the walk that I was about to walk. It has been a hard road. This road has had many places where I was sure I was about to call it quits, and I would go to the Lord in prayer and cry and say "*Why* Lord? Why me?" Then I would visit my core beliefs. "Jerilyn, what have you learned since accepting Jesus as your Savior? What does the word of God say? Do you believe that God is a healer? Do you really believe that God can intervene in this situation and turn it for your good?" You have a legal right to end this thing. You can find biblical backing for a decision to leave; this was adultery. You have placed yourself in place that you have no one who understands completely, but God. So what was my answer to these musings? Lord, I know you have a plan. *Please* help me; I don't see anything right now but the pain and hurt. Lord, I begged and pleaded with you in prayer to be married. Now I am married. Lord, I said out of my own mouth I only want to do this one time. Well, my talking has made a tough rough road for my walking. I got people looking at me calling me a *fool*. Lord, *help me*! I can truthfully say that the Word of God and his precious Holy Spirit have helped me. During the course of the past nine years, much healing has taken place in my life. And growth, growth that has literally catapulted me to walk a road full of adventure on this Christian Journey. I say adventure because now I ask, "Okay, Lord, how are you going to help me navigate this new challenge in front of me?" What's been the challenges? Too numerous to tell in this one sitting, but I will name a few. Number one, *forgiveness*; number two, *truth*; number three, *faithfulness*; number four, *having a fulfilling sex life*; number five, surviving the many trips to the hospital. And to conclude this list number six, to still have *joy* in the midst of my sorrow. Again, yes, this is a real-life, true story. We are still walking in a process of healing. We are still learning how to be one, just like anyone else in a marriage without this health issue. HIV/AIDS has almost become a seemingly normal disease with the new drugs that have been created, but it still has to be monitored, or you can *die*.

For me, the monitoring has happened in the word of God, making a daily decision to stick to the choice I made, keeping my heart and mind truly focused on what is God's plan for my life. And finally, expectancy, my heart is expectant/anticipating what's next. Yes, I go to the doctor on a regular basis. Yes, they check my counts to see where I am. Yes, they give me the doom gloom news of my "condition" every time they see me. But I have a song in my heart and a bite-the-inside-of-your mouth determination right there in front of the doctor, "I shall not die, *but live*, to declare the works of the Lord" (Psalm 118:17). It works, I am still here. I am *alive*! Oh, but for the *grace* of God. God bless you. I pray that as you have read this book, your life has been changed for the better. Don't question my choice; search yourself and see what your hard choices are in front of you. Will you make the right choice?

US Statistics on HIV/AIDS

Fast Facts

- More than 1.1 million people in the U.S. are living with HIV today, but 1 in 7 of them don't know it.
- An estimated 37,600 Americans became newly infected with HIV in 2014.
- From 2008 to 2014, the estimated number of annual HIV infections in the U.S. declined 18%.
- In 2016, 39,782 people were diagnosed with HIV in the U.S.
- Gay and bisexual men, particularly young African American gay and bisexual men, are most affected.
- Southern states bear the greatest burden of HIV, accounting for 50% of new infections in 2014.
- In the jurisdictions where they could be estimated, annual infections in all states decreased or remained stable from 2008-2014.

Estimated New HIV Infections
According to the latest estimates from the Centers for Disease Control and Prevention (CDC), an estimated 37,600 people became newly infected with HIV in the United States in 2014. Encouragingly, the estimated number of annual HIV infections in the U.S. declined 18% between 2008-2014 (from 45,700 to 37,600). Reductions were seen in most risk groups and in all states where data were available. Even greater reductions were observed among people who inject drugs (56% reduction) and heterosexual men and women (36%).

Gay and bisexual men were the only group that did not experience an overall decline in annual HIV infections from 2008 to 2014. This is because reduced infections among whites (18%) and the youngest gay and bisexual men (18%) were offset by increases in other groups. Annual infections remained stable at about 26,000 per year among gay and bisexual men overall and about 10,000 infections per year among black gay and bisexual men — a hopeful sign after more than a decade of increases in these populations. However, concerning trends emerged among gay and bisexual males of certain ages and ethnicities, with annual infections increasing: 35% among twenty-five to thirty four year-old gay and bisexual males (from 7,200 to 9,700) and 20% among Latino gay and bisexual males (from 6,100 to 7,300).

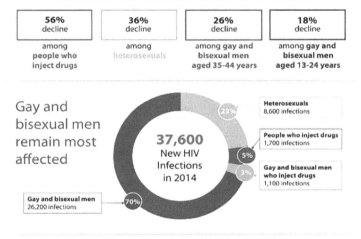

HIV Diagnoses[c]

In 2016, 39,782 people were diagnosed with HIV infection in the United States. The annual number of new HIV diagnoses fell 5% from 2011 to 2015. Because HIV testing has remained stable or increased in recent years, this decrease in diagnoses suggests a true decline in new infections. The decrease may be due to targeted HIV prevention efforts. However, progress has been uneven, and diagnoses have increased among a few groups.

Gay and bisexual men are the population most affected by HIV. In 2016d:

- Gay and bisexual men accounted for 67% (26,570) of all diagnoses and 83% of HIV diagnoses among males.
- Black/African American gay and bisexual men accounted for the largest number of HIV diagnoses (10,223), followed by Hispanic/Latino (7,425) and white (7,390) gay and bisexual men.

Among all gay and bisexual men, trends have varied by race and over time. From 2011 to 2015:

- Among white gay and bisexual men, diagnoses decreased 10%.
- Among Hispanic/Latin of gay and bisexual men, diagnoses increased 14%.

- Among African American gay and bisexual men, diagnoses increased 4%.
- After years of sharp increases, diagnoses among young African American gay and bisexual men (aged 13-24) stayed about the same.

Heterosexuals and people who inject drugs also continue to be affected by HIV. In 2016:

- Heterosexual contact accounted for 24% (9,578) of HIV diagnoses.
- Women accounted for 19% (7,529) of HIV diagnoses. Diagnoses among women are primarily attributed to heterosexual contact (87%, or 6,541) or injection drug use (12%, or 939).
- People who inject drugs accounted for 9% (3,425) of HIV diagnoses (includes 1,201 diagnoses among gay and bisexual men who inject drugs).

From 2011 to 2015:

- Diagnoses among all women declined 16%.
- Among all heterosexuals, diagnoses declined 15%, and among people who inject drugs, diagnoses declined 17%.

By race/ethnicity, **African Americans and Hispanics/Latinos** are disproportionately affected by HIV. In 2016:

- African Americans represented 12% of the U.S. population, but accounted for 44% (17,528) of HIV diagnoses. African Americans have the highest rate of HIV diagnoses compared to other races and ethnicities.
- Hispanics/Latinos represented about 18% of the U.S. population, but accounted for 25% (9,766) of HIV diagnoses.

New HIV Diagnoses in the United States for the Most-Affected Subpopulations, 2016

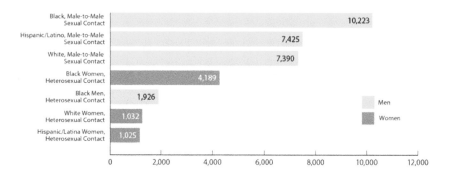

Source: Source: CDC. Diagnoses of HIV infection in the United States and dependent areas, 2016. HIV Surveillance Report 2017; 28.

Subpopulations representing 2% or less of HIV diagnoses are not reflected in this chart.

New HIV diagnoses also vary substantially by age:

New HIV Diagnoses in the United States by Age, 2016

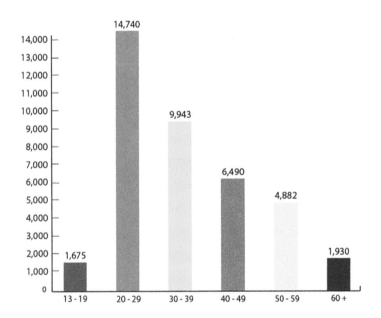

Source: CDC. Diagnoses of HIV infection in the United States and dependent areas, 2016. HIV Surveillance Report 2017; 28.

The burden of HIV and AIDS is not evenly distributed geographically. The population rates (per 100,000 people) of persons who received an HIV diagnosis were highest in the South (16.8), followed by the Northeast (11.2), the West (10.2), and the Midwest (7.5).g The South generally is behind other regions in some key HIV prevention and care indicators.

Living With HIV

- An estimated 1,122,900 adults and adolescents were living with HIV in the U.S. at the end of 2015.
- Of those, 162,500 (15% or 1 in 7) had not received a diagnosis, so were unaware of their infection.
- Young people were the most likely to be unaware of their infection. Among people aged 13-24 who were living with HIV, an estimated 44% didn't know.
- In 2014, among all adults and adolescents living with HIV (diagnosed or undiagnosed),

    o   62% received some HIV medical care,
    o   48% were retained in continuous HIV care, and
    o   49% had achieved viral suppression (having a very low level of the virus).h

A person living with HIV who takes HIV medicine as prescribed and gets and stays virally suppressed can stay healthy and has effectively no risk of sexually transmitting HIV to HIV-negative partners.

AIDS Diagnoses and Deaths

In 2016, 18,160 people received an AIDS diagnosis. Since the epidemic began in the early 1980s, 1,232,246 people have received an AIDS diagnosis.

In 2014, there were 12,333 deaths (due to any cause) of people with diagnosed HIV infection ever classified as AIDS, and 6,721 deaths were attributed directly to HIV.

Read more about the U.S. Government's domestic HIV/AIDS activities.

Notes

A. Thirty-five states and Washington, DC

B. The terms men who have sex with men and male-to-male sexual contact are used in CDC surveillance systems. They indicate a behavior that transmits HIV infection, not how individuals self-identify in terms of their sexuality. This page uses the term gay and bisexual men to include gay, bisexual, and other men who have sex with men, regardless of how they self-identify.

C. HIV and AIDS diagnoses refer to the estimated number of people diagnosed with HIV infection, regardless of stage of disease at diagnosis, and AIDS during a given time period.

D. These numbers include only diagnoses attributed to male-to-male sexual contact, not those attributed to injection drug use and male-to-male sexual contact.

E. Referred to as African American on this page.

F. Hispanics/Latinos can be of any race.

G. This page uses the regions defined by the U.S. Census Bureau and used in CDC's National HIV Surveillance System:

Northeast: CT, ME, MA, NH, NJ, NY, PA, RI, VT
Midwest: IL, IN, IA, KS, MI, MN, MO, NE, ND, OH, SD, WI
South: AL, AR, DE, DC, FL, GA, KY, LA, MD, MS, NC, OK, SC, TN, TX, VA, WV
West: AK, AZ, CA, CO, HI, ID, MT, NV, NM, OR, UT, WA, WY.

H. People are considered retained in care if they get two viral load or CD4 tests at least 3 months apart in a year. (CD4 cells are the cells in the body's immune system that are destroyed by HIV.) Viral suppression (having less than 200 copies of HIV per milliliter of blood) is based on the most recent viral load test.

Bibliography

CDC. HIV Surveillance Report, 2016; vol. 28. November 2017.

CDC. HIV Incidence: Estimated Annual Infections in the U.S., 2008 to 2014, Overall and by Transmission Route. February 2017.

CDC. Estimated New Infections in 2014, Nationally and by State. February 2017.

CDC. Diagnoses of HIV infection in the United States and dependent areas, 2015. HIV Surveillance Report 2016; 27.

CDC. Monitoring selected national HIV prevention and care objectives by using HIV surveillance data—United States and 6 dependent areas—2013. HIV Surveillance Supplemental Report 2015; 20(2).

CDC. State HIV prevention progress report, 2010-2013. December 2015.

CDC. Deaths: Final Data for 2014. National Vital Statistics Reports 2016; 65(4). Accessed November 21, 2016.

CDC. Trends in U.S. HIV diagnoses, 2005-2014 [fact sheet]. February 2016.

Content Source: HIV.gov
Date last updated: December 05, 2017

About the Authors

R obert and Jerilyn Ward met at church and were married in the summer of 1991, on July 30th, and have been married for twenty-seven years. They both have worked together diligently in ministry before and after getting married and did whatever God put into their hands to do. Three children were born into this union; Nicholas, Brea, and Jessica who have also worked alongside them in the ministry.

Robert and Jerilyn Ward are the pastors of In Spirit and In Truth Ministries International, Inc., which was launched in Deerfield Beach, Florida. Their ministry reaches out to broken marriages, families, and individuals that are trying to break free from the traditional mindsets that have kept them in bondage.

Isaiah 61:1–4

CPSIA information can be obtained
at www.ICGtesting.com
Printed in the USA
LVHW022229290419
616013LV00004B/47/P